"Best synthesis of cognitive science ever"
Mary Myatt, Education writer, speaker, founder Myatt & Co

"Visual learning at its best"
John Hattie, Melbourne Laureate Professor Emeritus, Melbourne Graduate School of Education. Author of bestselling *Visible Learning* series

"Absolutely illuminating"
Jenny Griffiths, Research and Knowledge Manager, Teach First

"Game changing"
Jade Pearce, Director of Programmes and author of *'What Every Teacher Needs to Know'*

"Seminal"
Henry Sauntson, Director Teach East SCITT

"Heavy concepts made incredibly accessible"
Lekha Sharma, Curriculum and Assessment Lead, Avanti Schools Trust

"Enlightening"
Dr Claire Badger, Assistant Head, Teaching and Learning, The Godolphin and Latymer School

"Complex research beautifully rendered"
Dr Carl Hendrick, author of *'How Learning Happens'*

"Expertly clarifies complex concepts"
Sarah Cottingham, MA Educational Neuroscience, Associate Dean at Ambition Institute.

"A warm bath for your brain"
Peps McCrea, Dean at Ambition Institute, Director at Steplab, Author of the *High Impact Teaching* series

"Infographabulous"
Paul Kirschner, Professor Emeritus Open University of the Netherlands, Guest Professor Thomas More University of Applied Sciences (Antwerp, Belgium), Owner kirschner-ED

"Pure gold for every teacher"
Darren Leslie, PT Teaching & Learning and host of the *Becoming Educated* podcast

"Exceptional!"
Rhiannon Rainbow, School Improvement Leader and Co-founder #GLTBookClub

"Visually stunning, intellectually stimulating"
Mark Roberts, Director of Research and English teacher, Carrickfergus Grammar School.

TEACHING & LEARNING ILLUMINATED

This exciting new book from the bestselling authors of *The Science of Learning* takes complex ideas around teaching and learning and makes them easy to understand and apply through beautifully illustrated graphics. Each concept is covered over a double-page spread, with a full-page graphic on one page and supportive text on the other. This unique combination of accessible images and clear explanations helps teachers navigate the key principles and understand how to best implement them in the classroom.

Distilling key findings and ideas for great evidence-based teaching from a broad range of contemporary studies, the book covers the research findings, ideas and applications from the most important and fundamental areas of teaching and learning including:

- Retrieval Practice
- Spacing
- Interleaving
- Cognitive Load Theory
- Rosenshine's Principles
- Feedback
- Resilience
- Metacognition

Written to support, inspire and inform teaching staff and those involved in leadership and CPD, *Teaching & Learning Illuminated* will transform readers' understanding of teaching and learning research.

Bradley Busch is the lead psychologist at InnerDrive, UK.

Edward Watson is the founder of InnerDrive, UK.

Ludmila Bogatchek is the creative lead at InnerDrive, UK.

TEACHING & LEARNING ILLUMINATED

The Big Ideas, Illustrated

Bradley Busch, Edward Watson and Ludmila Bogatchek

Routledge
Taylor & Francis Group

LONDON AND NEW YORK

Designed cover image: Ludmila Bogatchek

First published 2023
by Routledge
4 Park Square, Milton Park, Abingdon, Oxon, OX14 4RN

and by Routledge
605 Third Avenue, New York, NY 10158

Routledge is an imprint of the Taylor & Francis Group, an informa business

British Library Cataloguing-in-Publication Data
A catalogue record for this book is available from the British Library

ISBN: 978-1-032-36895-5 (hbk)
ISBN: 978-1-032-36896-2 (pbk)
ISBN: 978-1-003-33436-1 (ebk)

DOI: 10.4324/9781003334361

Typeset in Interstate
by Apex CoVantage, LLC

Printed in Great Britain by Bell and Bain Ltd, Glasgow

Because formatting is nine tenths of the message

ACKNOWLEDGEMENTS

BB: To Pippa, thank you for teaching me so much. To Jacob and Eli, I hope you both keep learning it all. To my parents, your constant support and belief is the foundation for everything I've done. And finally, to all my primary and secondary teachers, thank you for everything.

ETW: To Helen, Izzy and Ollie, thanks for putting up with my failings, for celebrating my successes and for being with me during the journey between the two. Thanks again to my darling wife for her love, support and wisdom. Thanks to my parents, teachers, friends and DC for making all this possible.

LB: Thanks to my dad for teaching me creativity, to my mum for teaching me conscientiousness and to Élise for giving me the teaching & learning bug.

From all of us, a big thank you to Routledge, for taking a chance on us again. Thanks to Luis Miguel who has illustrated our previous books and contributed to this one as well. Thank you to the many researchers and teachers whose work we have illuminated. We hope that we have done it the justice it deserves. And finally a big thank you to all the members of the InnerDrive team in particular to Matt, Nicky, Hanna, Tia, Tania, Emma and Patrick. It is a joy working with you all.

And of course, a big thank you to you, the reader, for supporting us and making it all worthwhile.

CONTENTS

How to read this book

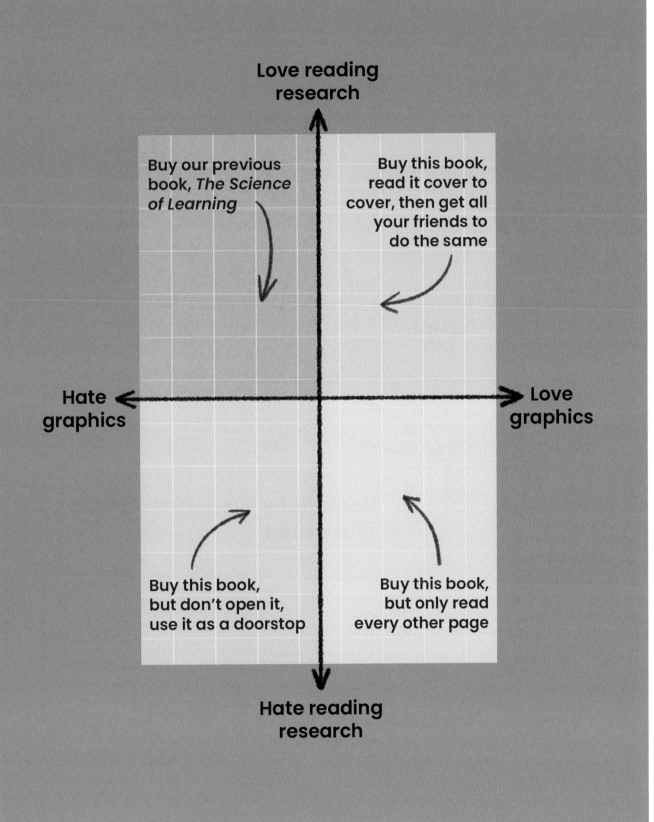

Love reading research

Buy our previous book, *The Science of Learning*

Buy this book, read it cover to cover, then get all your friends to do the same

Hate graphics

Love graphics

Buy this book, but don't open it, use it as a doorstop

Buy this book, but only read every other page

Hate reading research

What you'll get from *Teaching & Learning Illuminated*

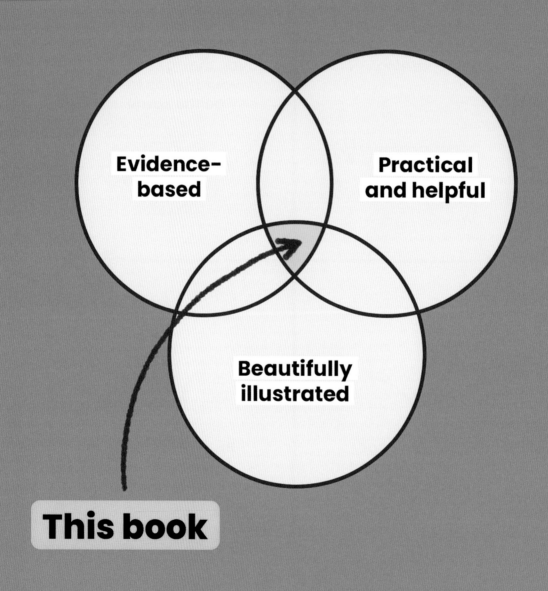

Evidence-based

Practical and helpful

Beautifully illustrated

This book

WHAT YOU'LL GET FROM *TEACHING & LEARNING ILLUMINATED*

Teaching & Learning is complicated, messy, nuanced and filled with caveats. The research is wide ranging, interlinked and at times incredibly complex and complicated. Even if we don't yet have definitive answers, we should take some comfort that nearly every big question in education has been at least partially researched. And there is gold in those research papers that can significantly help our students.

Unfortunately, there is a catch-22 that exists when discussing educational ideas and research. Often the original research can be filled with stats, jargon and intricate theory. To make this accessible, the presentation of this information needs to be adapted. But in doing so, we run the risk of dumbing down, misrepresenting and over-simplifying what the original research suggests. How then do we bridge this gap?

Professor, author and statistician Edward Tufte once famously declared that "there is no such thing as information overload, there is only bad design". We believe by presenting clear and beautiful graphics, we can capture the principles of this body of research elegantly. Indeed, as data-journalist and information designer David McCandless said, "by visualising information, we turn it into a landscape that you can explore with your eyes. A sort of information map. And when you're lost in information, an information map is kind of useful."

To this end, this book illustrates the research findings, ideas, concepts and applications on the most important and fundamental aspects of Teaching & Learning; including the likes of retrieval practice, spacing, interleaving, cognitive load theory, cognitive science, Rosenshine's Principles, feedback, resilience, motivation, metacognition, mobile phones and much more.

We read hundreds of peer-reviewed studies and spent thousand of hours trying to visually capture their essence. This book follows a simple format, with each concept covered over a double-page spread that starts with a graphic and is then supported with accompanying text. By marrying brilliant, deep and weighty educational and psychological research with beautiful illustrations, we hope this book leads to tangible and positive changes in your teaching.

Memory and Learning

Understanding <u>how students learn</u> is fundamental to <u>great teaching.</u>

DOI: 10.4324/9781003334361-1

Working memory vs long-term memory

Illuminated by @Inner_Drive | innerdrive.co.uk

Working memory is very small

This means that we forget new information quickly.

Long-term memory is very large

This means that we can remember things from years and years ago.

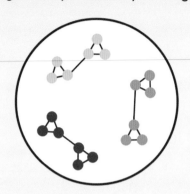

Transfer between working memory & long-term memory is key for learning

This can be facilitated through several strategies, such as Retrieval Practice.

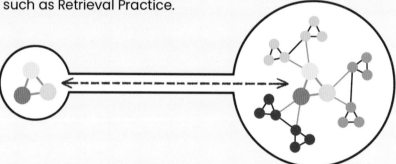

Unfortunately, cognitive overload hinders this transfer

This overload can be reduced through mitigating the Redundancy, Split-Attention and Transient Information Effects.

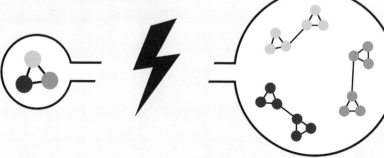

WORKING MEMORY VS LONG-TERM MEMORY

The fundamental principles of learning are built on the relationship between working memory and long-term memory. Working memory is where new information is processed. Unfortunately for students, it is small and has a limited capacity. This means it can easily become overwhelmed, with information quickly forgotten. To demonstrate just how small our working memory is, let's try an experiment. Without looking at the front cover, can you see if you can remember the spelling of the authors' surnames? Despite seeing that information only moments ago when you picked up this book, most people can't recall it with 100% accuracy.

And yet, our long-term memory is very large. In fact, it is probably impossible to quantify exactly how large it is. To give an indication of how vast it is, let's try another experiment. Can you recall what your favourite TV programme as a child was and what was the most popular song during your teenage years? Despite those memories being decades old, you can still retrieve that information from your long-term memory, as it is embedded in your brain.

A bi-directional relationship exists between working memory and long-term memory. Having a rich schema in our long-term memory means we free up space in our working memory, which helps us deduce where new pieces of information fit into the structure of what we already know.

Students do not always transfer information from their working memory to their long-term memory. This transfer matters for two reasons. First, if they do this, we can confidently say that they have truly learnt the material on a deep and meaningful level. Secondly, if we want them to be creative and innovative, then having this large bank of knowledge in the long-term memory enables them to use their working memory to manipulate this information in new and innovative ways.

Knowledge vs Awareness

Illuminated by @Inner_Drive | innerdrive.co.uk

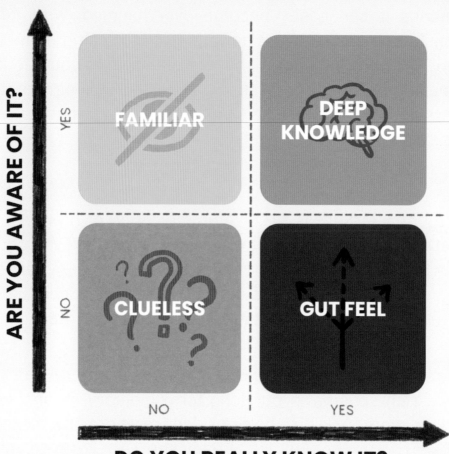

ARE YOU AWARE OF IT?

YES — FAMILIAR | DEEP KNOWLEDGE

NO — CLUELESS | GUT FEEL

NO | YES

DO YOU REALLY KNOW IT?

Familiar
Being aware of something but not really knowing it leads to familiarity and overconfidence.

Deep knowledge
Information sits in your long-term memory. You are able to easily recall it when needed.

Clueless
Beyond your knowledge. Not only do you not know the answer, you don't even understand the question.

Gut feel
It might be hard to articulate why you think X and not Y, but you feel that you know the right answer.

KNOWLEDGE VS AWARENESS

What is needed to have concrete deep knowledge of something? To borrow from Donald Rumsfeld's infamous explanation, how aware are you of something and do you really know about it?

One of the aims of teaching is to get students from the left boxes to the top right one. When students are brand new to a topic, the information they are about to learn may be far removed from their existing knowledge. This means they may not be able to make any meaningful connections. Simply telling students about something will get them from the bottom left box to the top left box, as their awareness of the topic grows.

However, awareness of a topic is not enough. Mistaking awareness for deep knowledge can lead to overconfidence. Because they are aware of the information when they see it, they are prone to overestimating how likely they are to remember it later from memory. This can lead to blind spots, where they don't revisit material as part of their learning, as they incorrectly feel that they will remember it. This is partially why inefficient techniques such as only re-reading their notes or highlighting key parts of the text are problematic.

When students are both aware of something and really know it, we can say it is deep knowledge. To help transfer information into this top right box, we need to use effective learning strategies (such as retrieval and spaced learning). Assessing if students know and remember more can be tricky. This is because memories change and fade over time. Therefore, we can make a judgement call on this if students can recall information, explain it in their own words, elaborate on it, apply it to different settings and do so repeatedly over time.

Best bets for learning

Illuminated by @Inner_Drive | innerdrive.co.uk

HIGH UTILITY

- Retrieval Practice
- Spacing

These are our best bets for learning

MEDIUM UTILITY

- Interleaving
- Elaborative Interrogation

LOW UTILITY

- Highlighting
- Re-reading
- Mnemonics
- Visualising
- Summarising

These can lead to the illusion of learning

Reference: Dunlosky et al, 2013

BEST BETS FOR LEARNING

Can we ever be confident that we know for sure what works when it comes to improving memory and learning? This question has been explored by practitioners and researchers alike for hundreds of years. Perhaps this is the wrong question to be asking. Instead, it is probably better to think of "best bets" or "general guidelines" instead. Doing so allows us to factor in nuance, context and future research that may change our minds.

The general consensus from cognitive science research is that Retrieval Practice and Spacing are what we should be hanging our hat on. Retrieval Practice is the act of deliberately recalling information, often done through questioning of some sort. Spacing is the act of revisiting material regularly. The latter is important as students tend to forget things at a quicker rate than most people realise.

So, if those are the best bets, what are the riskier ones? What strategies tend to provide minimal bang for their buck? Unfortunately, they tend to be the most popular ones amongst students: re-reading their notes and highlighting them. The problem with both of these strategies is that they can be done on autopilot. It is easy to skim read through whole sections of the material. It is possible to brainlessly and aimlessly highlight passages of text. Both, to the untrained eye, give the illusion of learning. But measuring learning by how many pages have been read or how many sections have been highlighted can give a false impression and lead to blind spots in one's knowledge.

If we are going to help students maximise their learning, then it is not enough for us as educators to be the only ones armed with this knowledge. We have to explicitly teach effective strategies for the acquisition of deep knowledge, if we are to get long-term and sustained behaviour change with regard to learning.

4 counterintuitive concepts on how we learn

By Sarah Cottingham | Illuminated by @Inner_Drive | innerdrive.co.uk

1. To increase expertise, don't do as the experts do

Do: Learn how to be an expert

Don't: Try to do what experts do

Novice → Expert

... so, build domain-specific knowledge in chunks and use modelling and scaffolding.

2. Pupils don't learn what you teach them

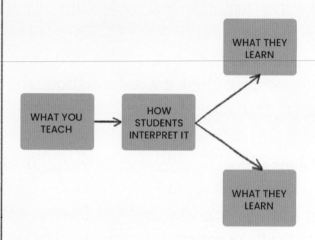

WHAT YOU TEACH → HOW STUDENTS INTERPRET IT → WHAT THEY LEARN / WHAT THEY LEARN

... so regularly check for understanding, link new material to what they know, and share common misconceptions.

3. Pupils' performance may not be a good indicator of learning

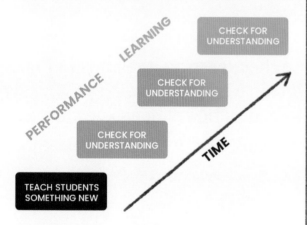

PERFORMANCE LEARNING

CHECK FOR UNDERSTANDING
CHECK FOR UNDERSTANDING
CHECK FOR UNDERSTANDING
TEACH STUDENTS SOMETHING NEW
TIME

... so check learning over long periods of time and use Retrieval Practice, Spacing and Interleaving.

4. Skills are built on domain-specific knowledge

What people see publicly

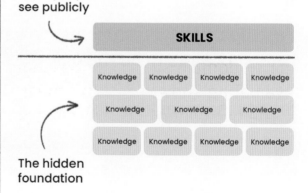

SKILLS

Knowledge | Knowledge | Knowledge | Knowledge
Knowledge | Knowledge | Knowledge
Knowledge | Knowledge | Knowledge | Knowledge

The hidden foundation

... so avoid teaching general "critical thinking". Build knowledge and get students to apply it in different ways.

4 COUNTERINTUITIVE CONCEPTS ON HOW WE LEARN

The problem: learning takes place in the brains of our pupils. We can't see it. We can only make inferences based on what our pupils say and do. A faulty understanding of learning means a faulty conception of how we should teach.

It's tempting to look to the end goal of learning and try to get pupils to imitate that. This would mean describing what an "expert" in a subject does and setting pupils tasks to copy the expert. If the end goal is that pupils can transfer their knowledge across topics, so they can answer exam questions and use this knowledge in the future, then the tasks they need to build this knowledge won't mirror exam questions, at least not at first.

Likewise, the meaning pupils make from what you say is a combination of what you say (or at least the bits they attend to) and the relevant knowledge they already have. Each pupil will use at least slightly different knowledge to understand what you say. This means the resultant meaning made by each pupil will be *at least* slightly different. In other words, once you've explained something new to pupils, you have 30 different interpretations sitting in front of you.

Because students learn their interpretation of what you teach, not what you actually taught, it is imperative to regularly check for understanding. Doing so can help avoid surface level "performance" and accurately gauge deeper long-term learning.

This long-term knowledge provides the platform for developing skills. By building up rich domain-specific knowledge, we can get students to practise applying and evaluating knowledge. This means that skills are us practising using knowledge. The two cannot be divorced from one another.

Note: A version of this page first appeared on the InnerDrive website, in a blog that Sarah Cottingham wrote for us. We would like to thank her not only for her incredible knowledge on the topic, but also for her generosity in letting us slightly adapt her work here.

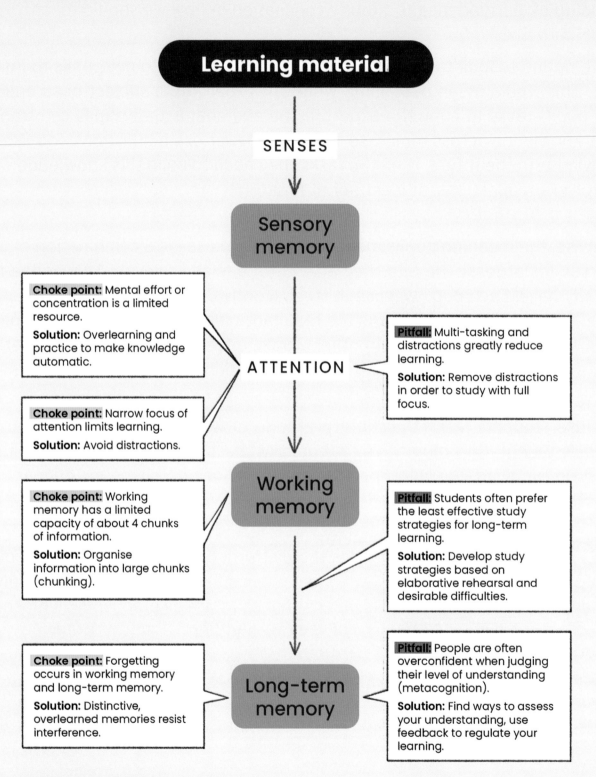

Choke points and pitfalls in learning

Created by Professor Chew | Illuminated by @Inner_Drive

Learning material

SENSES

Sensory memory

Choke point: Mental effort or concentration is a limited resource.

Solution: Overlearning and practice to make knowledge automatic.

Pitfall: Multi-tasking and distractions greatly reduce learning.

Solution: Remove distractions in order to study with full focus.

ATTENTION

Choke point: Narrow focus of attention limits learning.

Solution: Avoid distractions.

Working memory

Choke point: Working memory has a limited capacity of about 4 chunks of information.

Solution: Organise information into large chunks (chunking).

Pitfall: Students often prefer the least effective study strategies for long-term learning.

Solution: Develop study strategies based on elaborative rehearsal and desirable difficulties.

Long-term memory

Choke point: Forgetting occurs in working memory and long-term memory.

Solution: Distinctive, overlearned memories resist interference.

Pitfall: People are often overconfident when judging their level of understanding (metacognition).

Solution: Find ways to assess your understanding, use feedback to regulate your learning.

Reference: Chew, 2021

CHOKE POINTS AND PITFALLS IN LEARNING

This graphic was originally designed by Professor Stephen Chew, a professor of psychology at Samford University, in his research paper titled "Chokepoints and Pitfalls in Studying". In it, he concisely and expertly highlights the many barriers that students face when learning new information. In order to do so, he divides these barriers into two distinct and yet related sections: Choke Points and Pitfalls.

A Choke Point is a naturally occurring limitation within human cognitive architecture. For example, this includes how hard it is to focus intensely over long periods of time, how our working memory has a limited capacity and how difficult it is to transfer information from working memory through to long-term memory.

A Pitfall on the other hand is a faulty belief that students have about how the learning process works. Examples include their belief that they can multi-task effectively, or their overconfidence that they will remember information for long periods of time. Another pitfall is the difference between how they prefer to study and what is actually most effective.

By noting both the choke points and the pitfalls, it allows us to better plan our lessons and spot potential for misunderstanding, confusion and general forgetting. For example, if we know students are likely to overestimate how much they will remember in the future, we can factor in time to revisit information. Likewise, once we fully appreciate just how much of a myth conscious multi-tasking is, we can look to remove potential distractions. This could well be the first step we take in helping students manage their cognitive load.

We do not consider this list to be exhaustive. No doubt, other choke points and pitfalls exist. This may include areas around the role motivation and emotions play in the learning process. However, thinking in these terms allows us to tailor our teaching with the students' brain in mind.

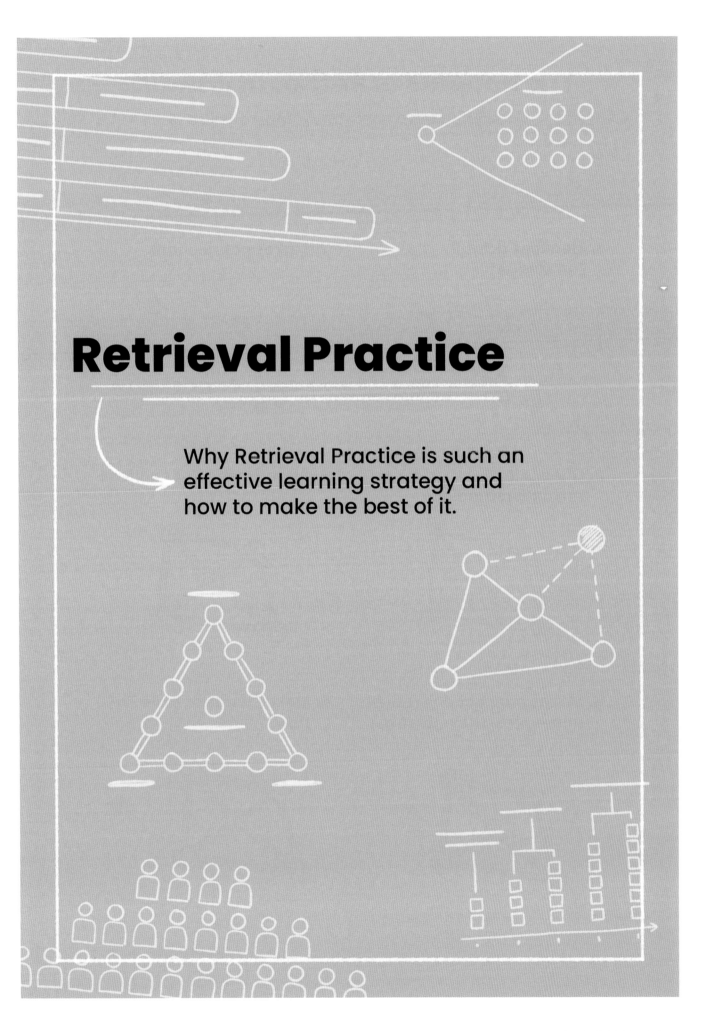

Retrieval Practice

Why Retrieval Practice is such an effective learning strategy and how to make the best of it.

DOI: 10.4324/9781003334361-2

The benefits of Retrieval Practice

Illuminated by @Inner_Drive | innerdrive.co.uk

1. Identifies gaps in knowledge

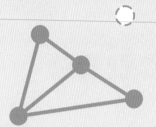

2. Makes connections

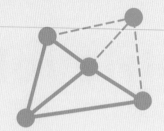

3. Checks for misunderstandings

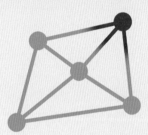

4. Strengthens connections

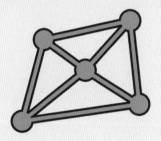

5. Makes connections robust under pressure and stress

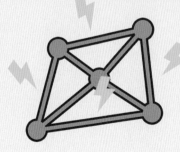

6. Makes it easier to learn new things

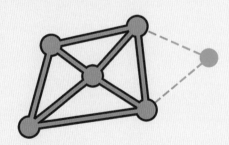

THE BENEFITS OF RETRIEVAL PRACTICE

Retrieval Practice can take many different forms, such as low-stakes quizzing, multiple-choice tests, flashcards, mini-whiteboards, past papers or even verbal question + answer. Decades' worth of research findings, which have been consistently replicated, have found it to be very effective. But what are the mechanisms that underpin it?

The first is that it helps students identify existing gaps in this knowledge. If they are unable to successfully retrieve information, it can be an indicator of what they do or don't know. The second benefit is that it can help them make connections. This is because retrieving is a cognitively demanding task. In doing so, it helps embed and cement information. This consolidation and interconnection of ideas will help them build rich schemas of knowledge.

Unfortunately, memory is not permanent. The brain is constantly editing and rewiring, which means over time misunderstandings can develop. Regular retrieval practice can help guard against this. As well as memory editing, it also fades. One round of retrieval practice is not enough to secure the memory long term. Using a range of different retrieval practice strategies over time can help strengthen our current existing connections.

When we are stressed, our focus of attention narrows, meaning we find it harder to retain and recall information. This is why exam pressure can sometimes hinder student performance. And yet, evidence suggests that when students study using retrieval practice, it creates a buffer. This means that they find it easier to remember key information when it matters most.

The final benefit is one that applies to memory in general. Evidence suggests that the more we know, the easier it is to learn new information, as essentially, we have more anchor points to hook the new information on to. Given that retrieval practice is a very effective way to cement information into our long-term memory, it stands to reason that doing so provides a firm foundation for future learning.

How do students feel about Retrieval Practice?

Illuminated by @Inner_Drive | innerdrive.co.uk

After using Retrieval Practice, do students feel less anxious, the same, or more anxious?

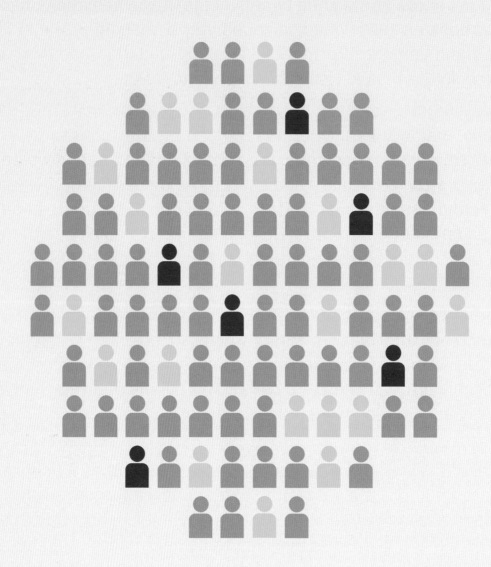

Reference: Agarwal et al, JARMAC, 2014 | @retrievelearn

HOW DO STUDENTS FEEL ABOUT RETRIEVAL PRACTICE?

Multiple studies have found that retrieval practice aids learning. It would therefore be a good guess to assume that students often choose to use it. However, their relationship with retrieval practice is a bit more complicated than that.

Despite its effectiveness, retrieval practice is not the method of choice for most students when it comes to their studying. Evidence from several studies has found that, given the choice, students prefer re-reading their notes. This is because it is safe, comfortable and never forces them to confront what they do or don't know. Their short-term self-esteem remains intact. The downside is that it also gives a false sense of confidence in what they actually know.

The study that this graphic is based on asked students how they felt after they used retrieval practice in preparation for their upcoming exams. So it seems that once we have actually got them doing it, even though they may not intuitively choose it themselves, the vast majority feel much better for it. This suggests that instead of just telling them the benefits of it (though this probably would help a little), the best route to convincing them is just to get them doing it. Then they will see and feel the benefits for themselves.

There is no denying that students have an uncomfortable relationship with retrieval practice, at least to start with. It's mentally taxing and by design uncovers gaps in knowledge. So you can see why students may be reluctant to choose it themselves when working independently. And yet if we can push past that initial resistance, they tend to feel much better for it.

Retrieval Practice in the classroom

Illuminated by @Inner_Drive | innerdrive.co.uk

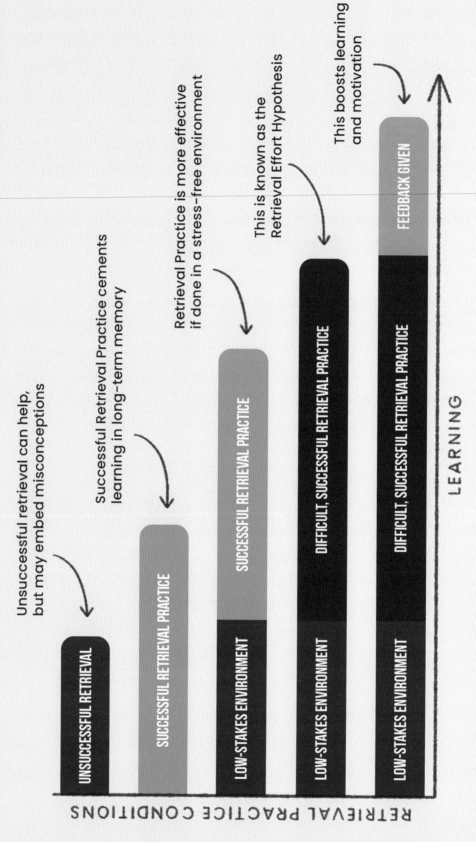

Unsuccessful retrieval can help, but may embed misconceptions

Successful Retrieval Practice cements learning in long-term memory

Retrieval Practice is more effective if done in a stress-free environment

This is known as the Retrieval Effort Hypothesis

This boosts learning and motivation

FEEDBACK GIVEN

UNSUCCESSFUL RETRIEVAL

SUCCESSFUL RETRIEVAL PRACTICE

LOW-STAKES ENVIRONMENT / SUCCESSFUL RETRIEVAL PRACTICE

LOW-STAKES ENVIRONMENT / DIFFICULT, SUCCESSFUL RETRIEVAL PRACTICE

LOW-STAKES ENVIRONMENT / DIFFICULT, SUCCESSFUL RETRIEVAL PRACTICE

RETRIEVAL PRACTICE CONDITIONS

LEARNING

RETRIEVAL PRACTICE IN THE CLASSROOM

The weight of evidence around the principle that retrieval aids learning is considerable. What is less well known, and still currently being explored, is the conditions under which it works best in the classroom. This is because classrooms are much more complicated than research labs.

That being said, some evidence-based guidelines are beginning to emerge. The first is that for retrieval practice to be effective, it needs to be "low stakes". This means done in a non-stressful and non-judgemental way. Arguably this is the core difference between a "test" and a "quiz". (The waters were somewhat muddied here as many people refer to retrieval practice as "the testing effect", whereas a more apt name would have been "the quizzing effect".)

A low-stakes environment can be induced by making retrieval practice a standard norm of the classroom, as opposed to a big one-off event. Likewise, removing leader boards, timers or anything else that is likely to increase stress or fear of failure will help.

The "retrieval effort hypothesis" suggests that if retrieval is too easy, it is not likely to be very effective. Part of the value in retrieval is getting students to think hard about the material. There is probably a sweet spot to be found here, almost like the Goldilocks effect, where if it is too easy then it isn't demanding enough, and if it is too hard it can be demoralising. Therefore, the mantra of "difficult but successful" offers a good philosophy.

Retrieval practice can still be beneficial if it is unsuccessful. Evidence suggests that it can help activate surrounding schemas, as well as increasing curiosity, attention and motivation. However, the risk is that incorrect answers that were retrieved may be remembered. It appears that under this condition, timely feedback from the teacher is key.

Retrieval Practice does not exist in a vacuum

Illuminated by @Inner_Drive | innerdrive.co.uk

The Retrieval Practice and feedback loop

Retrieval Practice — Roediger III et al, 2011 → Feedback

Feedback — Hui et al, 2021 → Retrieval Practice

Retrieval Practice, Metacognition and learning

Naujoks et al, 2022

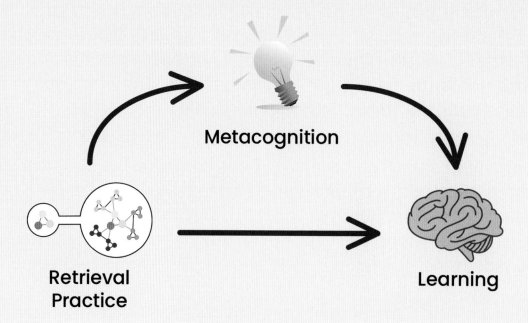

Retrieval Practice → Metacognition → Learning

Retrieval Practice → Learning

RETRIEVAL PRACTICE DOES NOT EXIST IN A VACUUM

There is a very curious relationship that exists between retrieval practice and feedback. The first, and most obvious, aspect is that engaging with retrieval practice can lead to students having a healthier and more proactive relationship with feedback. Regardless as to whether students successfully retrieve some information, it can lead to them getting feedback (either confirming what they got right or corrective feedback on what they got wrong). This feedback could focus on either the content, or the thought process/strategy they used.

We can therefore see how retrieval practice can provide a foundation for improving self-awareness. By having an accurate view of what they do and don't know, students can then target their future study efforts more accurately. This is one of the foundations upon which metacognition is built. Without this self-awareness, students are more prone to stumbling from one task to the next, without ever reflecting on what would help develop their knowledge best.

As well as retrieval practice driving feedback, the reverse is also true. One recent study found that students who had received feedback after they used retrieval practice were more likely to use retrieval practice again in the future; a positive loop of retrieval–feedback–retrieval is created.

Another fascinating recent study found that when retrieval practice is combined with feedback, it significantly enhances student motivation. Tapping in to student motivation is obviously a key part of the learning process, so we can start to see how these key areas all interlink.

One possible reason why this retrieval practice + feedback combination increases motivation is that as well as raising student confidence level, it more importantly raises their competence levels. Confidence is often a consequence of competence, with research suggesting that prior achievement is a strong predictor of self-efficacy. Confidence without competence tends not to last. Therefore, by helping them get better at the task, we also make students feel better about it too.

Designing the perfect multiple-choice test

Illuminated by @Inner_Drive | innerdrive.co.uk

Structure of the question

AVOID:

Complex questions lead to misunderstandings and students just guess the answer.

USE:

Simple and clear questions maximise the chance of targeted Retrieval Practice.

Number of potential answers

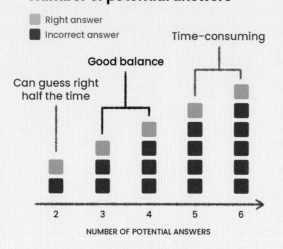

- Right answer
- Incorrect answer

Time-consuming

Good balance

Can guess right half the time

2   3   4   5   6

NUMBER OF POTENTIAL ANSWERS

Avoid really easy answers

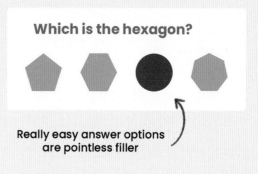

Which is the hexagon?

Really easy answer options are pointless filler

Aim for 70-80% success

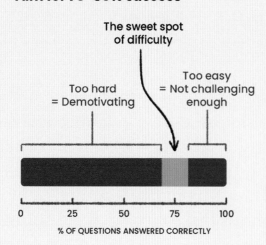

The sweet spot of difficulty

Too easy = Not challenging enough

Too hard = Demotivating

0   25   50   75   100

% OF QUESTIONS ANSWERED CORRECTLY

Avoid using "None of the above"

What makes a good multiple-choice question?

○ Complex questions
○ Many potential answers
○ One really easy answer
○ None of the above

If "None of the above" is the right answer, students have been exposed to wrong answers and don't get to retrieve the correct answer

Reference: Butler, 2018

DESIGNING THE PERFECT MULTIPLE-CHOICE TEST

Given how important retrieval is to the learning process, multiple-choice questions have seen an increase in popularity in the classroom. But what makes a good multiple-choice question?

Research now offers the following guidelines. The first is to avoid using complex questions or complex answer formats. When things are too complex, it leads to misunderstandings and students guess the answer. By keeping the format simple, it makes it a more reliable assessment of what the students do or don't know. Essentially, it is a better test of their knowledge.

We should also consider the number of answer options. If we only give two options, then students can guess right 50% of the time without any prior knowledge. This is a poor form of retrieval, as it is more akin to tossing a coin. Likewise, giving too many answer options becomes quite time-heavy, meaning less of a range of topics can be covered in the questions. This suggests 3 or 4 answer options tend to offer the best blend.

It is also good to avoid really obvious wrong answers. These are pointless fillers. Each answer choice should be "moderately difficult". This is also in sync with the intended overall success-rate of the multiple-choice test. Various researchers and practitioners seem to congregate around the 75% level. Any higher and the quiz isn't challenging enough to maximise retrieval, and if it is significantly lower it can be demoralising.

Finally, it may be wise to consider avoiding using "None of the above" as an option. The main issue with "None of the above" is that if it is the correct answer, then the test-taker has been exposed to numerous false answers. This represents a missed opportunity to reinforce what the correct answer is.

Taking multiple-choice tests to the next level

Illuminated by @Inner_Drive | innerdrive.co.uk

Confidence-weighted multiple-choice questions lead to wider retrieval and deeper learning.

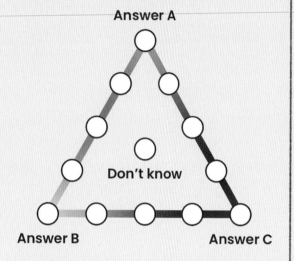

Multiple-choice questions can prompt whole class reflective feedback and discussion.

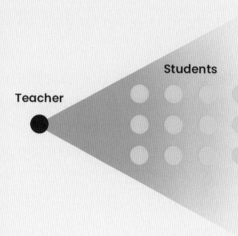

Good multiple-choice questions use each incorrect answer to target specific misconceptions and faulty thought processes.

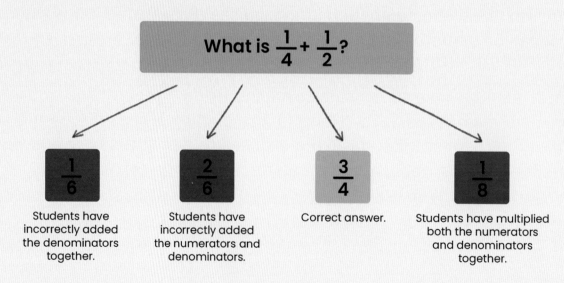

What is $\frac{1}{4} + \frac{1}{2}$?

$\frac{1}{6}$
Students have incorrectly added the denominators together.

$\frac{2}{6}$
Students have incorrectly added the numerators and denominators.

$\frac{3}{4}$
Correct answer.

$\frac{1}{8}$
Students have multiplied both the numerators and denominators together.

TAKING MULTIPLE-CHOICE TESTS TO THE NEXT LEVEL

Confidence-weighted multiple-choice questions, which is where students can indicate how confident they are on each answer, has the potential to help students engage in a deeper thinking process. This is because it taps into a wider range of retrieval, as well as discourages guessing, as there is an "I don't know" option. As a result, evidence suggests that students who take these sorts of tests are more likely to be able to answer new but related questions later on.

It is worth noting that standard multiple-choice tests are easier to administer and mark than confidence-weighted ones. This should be factored into the decision as to if/how regularly to use them in the classroom. As with all strategies based on research, it is not just the potential impact that matters, but it is the impact divided by time or cost taken to implement that truly counts.

As well as engaging in specific and direct retrieval practice, one of the other benefits of using multiple-choice questions is that it can help identify faulty thought processes. Once identified, these can then be targeted to be corrected later on. For this to be as effective as possible, each potential answer should target a specific misconception. As students from each year group typically experience the same type of misunderstanding or misconceptions, these can often be predicted in advance. Overall, this means that the incorrect answers in multiple-choice tests are not just mere distractors, but are prompts that can help guide future teaching.

Another powerful perspective to consider multiple-choice tests from is what happens after students complete the test. Evidence suggests that using it as a foundation for whole-class discussion and feedback can further accelerate learning. Although this may potentially take up a considerable amount of extra time, it allows students to learn from both their own and each other's mistakes.

Spacing and Interleaving

The importance of regularly reviewing information, as well as comparing and contrasting it.

DOI: 10.4324/9781003334361-3

Cramming vs Spacing

Created by Carl Hendrick & Oliver Caviglioli
Illuminated by @Inner_Drive | innerdrive.co.uk

CRAMMING VS SPACING

The "Spacing Effect" is one of the longest and most enduring findings in cognitive psychology. It was first detailed in 1885 by German psychologist Hermann Ebbinghaus who found that humans tend to forget large amounts of information if they only learn something once. Looking back, his study was pretty revolutionary, and as a result of the rigorous scientific method he employed, the results of his research are still being replicated over one hundred years later.

Since then, research has consistently shown the power of spacing our learning. This means doing little and often, instead of a lot all at once. For example, it is probably more effective for long-term learning to do one hour of learning a day for seven days than it is to do seven hours in one day.

Spacing has consistently been found to be one of the best learning strategies, with a good number of studies finding a 10–30% improvement in memory retention. This is because to commit something to memory takes both time and repetition. Quite counterintuitively, one of the reasons why spacing works is because it allows time to almost forget the content before re-learning it. Each time we almost forget and then re-learn, we cement and ingrain the information deeper into our long-term memory.

Another benefit of spacing, alongside the improvement to memory and learning, is that it is less stressful. Having to cram learning into one session just before an exam isn't conducive to mental well-being. The extra stress and intensity of an already stressful event adds unnecessary extra pressure to it.

Researchers have tried to find the optimum amount of time to leave between revisiting content, but have been unable to come up with a definitive answer. This is because there are so many factors to consider, but as a rough rule of thumb, the general rule appears to be that the longer you want to remember something for, the longer the gaps between sessions need to be.

Blocking

Blocking involves doing concept 1, then concept 2, then concept 3.

Interleaving

Interleaving involves mixing up concepts within a topic.

Why it works:

1. Discrimination learning: Spotting **differences between similar things**

When students think about differences, we prompt them to think harder. Contrasting information is more likely to stick in our mind.

2. Involves remembering **similarities between different things**

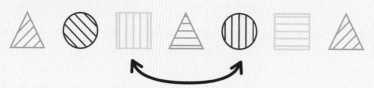

By highlighting similarities between different things, we provide more "anchor points" for students to hook new information onto.

3. Involves the **benefits of Spacing**

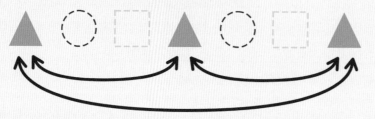

Each time the information is revisited, it helps ingrain and cement it into our long-term memory.

WHY INTERLEAVING WORKS

Interleaving is often linked to spacing, but although there is an element of spacing within it, interleaving is a standalone strategy. Some researchers believe that some of the difference lies in that spacing relies on mentally recharging between learning sessions to help slow down the forgetting rate, which helps replenish cognitive effort. Interleaving draws more heavily on contrasting between different concepts.

Interleaving involves the mixing up of concepts within a topic. The opposite of interleaving is blocking, which is fully covering one concept, before moving on to the next and then the next. Research suggests that interleaving can help significantly boost learning and memory. But why is this the case? Three possible reasons have been offered.

The first is called "discrimination learning", which describes how when students spot the differences between similar things, they tend to remember the content more. This is not too dissimilar to the "contrast" part of "compare and contrast between two things". By viewing two different things in close proximity to each other, the differences become more apparent. This doesn't happen with blocking, either because students are more likely to be working on autopilot at the end of their blocking period (due to the familiarity with the content) or because they will forget what they had previously studied due to limitations of memory (i.e. we tend to forget things at a much faster rate than we realise).

The second benefit of interleaving is it helps students group similar things together. This allows them to identify trends, rules and concepts that complement each other. Doing so creates more "anchor points" that they can latch new information onto.

The third and final reason why interleaving can help is because it does involve an element of spacing. By definition, by comparing two or more concepts, we automatically space them out. So although distinct from spacing, it still has some elements of it.

The dos and don'ts of Interleaving

Illuminated by @Inner_Drive | innerdrive.co.uk

Don't: Interleave subjects instead of concepts

MATHS ENGLISH SCIENCE MATHS ENGLISH SCIENCE MATHS ENGLISH SCIENCE

Don't: Interleave too many concepts

1 2 3 4 5 6 1 2 3 4 5 6

Don't: Leave too long between interleaving

1 2 3 1 2 3 1 2 3

Larger gaps make it hard to make connections between concepts

If the gap is too long, too much forgetting happens

Do: Master the basics first, choose a few related concepts, and leave consistent gaps

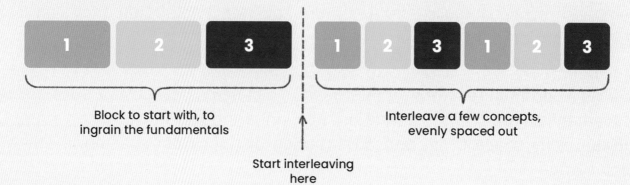

1 2 3 1 2 3 1 2 3

Block to start with, to ingrain the fundamentals

Start interleaving here

Interleave a few concepts, evenly spaced out

THE DOS AND DON'TS OF INTERLEAVING

Out of all the areas of cognitive science, interleaving is the one that many teachers tell us they struggle to implement the most. So what are the most common misconceptions, misunderstandings and myths about interleaving?

The first is with regard to what material one interleaves. Interleaving is not about mixing up the order of subjects (though arguably this would still benefit from a spacing effect). Interleaving is about mixing up the order of concepts within a topic. This means instead of mixing up Maths, English and Science, one would interleave three types of maths problems.

Another interleaving error is to try to interleave too many concepts at the same time. As discussed earlier, one of the benefits of interleaving is being able to distinguish and discriminate between similar concepts. If we try to compare and contrast too many different items of information, this will likely lead to a cognitive overload, as students' working memory becomes flooded with too much for them to process. It is interesting to note that there does not appear to be a consensus on what the optimal number of concepts to interleave is, though a number of studies do seem to limit it to about three at any one time.

One of the key benefits of interleaving is that it can help students make connections or contrasts between topics. It therefore is a mistake to leave too long between interleaved sessions. Another problem that arises with long gaps is that our memories themselves are not stable. They are subject to change and modification, as well as eventually fading. Leaving short gaps between interleaved sessions is best.

The final common mistake that occurs with interleaving is rushing to interleave at the beginning. Too much interleaving, before the basics have been mastered, can create problems further down the line. This can feel overwhelming and frustrating, as it can feel that nothing has been learnt due to the inconsistency of material being studied. Instead it is better to nail the fundamentals before interleaving a few concepts with small spaced gaps between them.

Spacing and interleaving for long-lasting learning

Illuminated by @Inner_Drive | innerdrive.co.uk

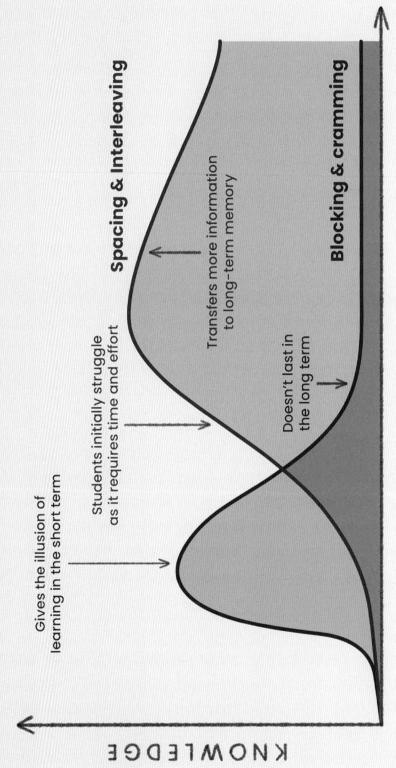

Spacing & interleaving

Gives the illusion of learning in the short term

Students initially struggle as it requires time and effort

Transfers more information to long-term memory

Doesn't last in the long term

Blocking & cramming

KNOWLEDGE

T I M E

* This infographic is not intended to reflect exact data points from a specific study. It is a visual representation of our interpretation of several studies combined.

One of the purposes of education is to help develop real and deep knowledge. This is the type of information that is remembered for long periods of time, can be applied to different settings and can be built upon. Shallower learning, although easier and quicker to attain, is much more likely to be forgotten.

Shallow learning, which results from blocking (doing one topic, then another, then another) and cramming (doing lots in one session) can give the illusion of learning. If we assess students straight after they do blocking or cramming they often score highly. This is because they are just repeating back the last thing they remember. This parroting back of information leads to a false sense of confidence.

Anything you can gain quickly you tend to lose quickly too. Memory is no different. Numerous studies have found that when students are asked to recall information a week or two after they do blocking or cramming, the amount they have forgotten is incredibly high.

We know that a lot of students initially struggle with interleaving. It requires hard work and in the short term is unlikely to yield impressive results. However, this type of learning is more "sticky", meaning the memory decay is much slower. This means it has more chance of being transferred into their long-term memory.

This graphic is not taken from one particular study. Instead, it reflects our general understanding of how different learning strategies impact students' ability to recall information over time. There may well be a time and place for some blocking, but what is undeniable is that students forget information quickly if they do not revisit it and if they do not make connections between what they are studying and what they already know. This means that Spacing and Interleaving are good strategies to help develop real deep knowledge.

1. Create 5 different boxes to store your flashcards. Start with all your flashcards in box 1.

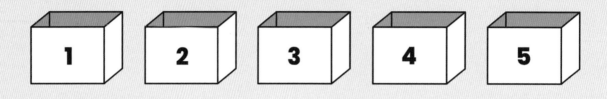

2. Every time you answer a flashcard correctly, move it to the next box. The time gap to revisit the flashcards increases with each subsequent box.

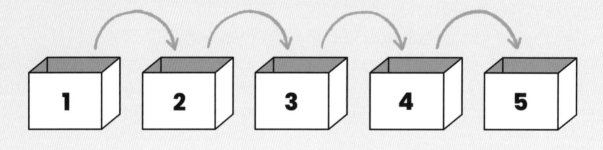

3. Every time you answer a flashcard incorrectly, move it back to the first box.

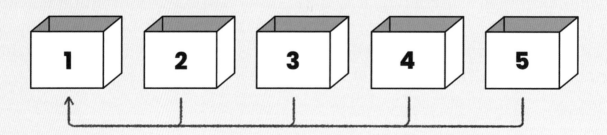

HOW TO USE THE LEITNER SYSTEM

So far we have covered the importance of Retrieval Practice, Spacing and Interleaving. But what if there was a system that students could use when they study independently that combines all three? Step forward the "Leitner System". Named after its creator, Sebastian Leitner, this system was first proposed in his book *So lernt man lernen* ("That's how you learn to learn") in the 1970s. This approach is arguably the most effective way for students to use flashcards.

The Leitner System uses a five-step process using flashcards and a "learning box". The box is separated into five different compartments labelled 1-5. All the flashcards start in compartment 1. When all the information is remembered from a card and the student can answer questions about it, the card moves to the next compartment.

Each time a flashcard is answered correctly, it moves to the next compartment. Each time it is answered incorrectly it moves back to the beginning (i.e. compartment number 1). This allows students to regularly quiz themselves on information that they have not yet embedded into their long-term memory.

There is no set time to leave between using each compartment. It can be flexible depending on the learner. One strategy could be reviewing the first compartment daily, with the second compartment being reviewed every other day, compartment 3 being reviewed every third day, compartment 4 once a week and compartment 5 once a fortnight.

The Leitner System utilises a concept called Spaced Repetition. It helps students regularly revisit material that they may otherwise have forgotten, and in doing so prompts them to retrieve and recall the information. The more they do so, the less likely they are to forget, and the longer they can leave before revisiting it.

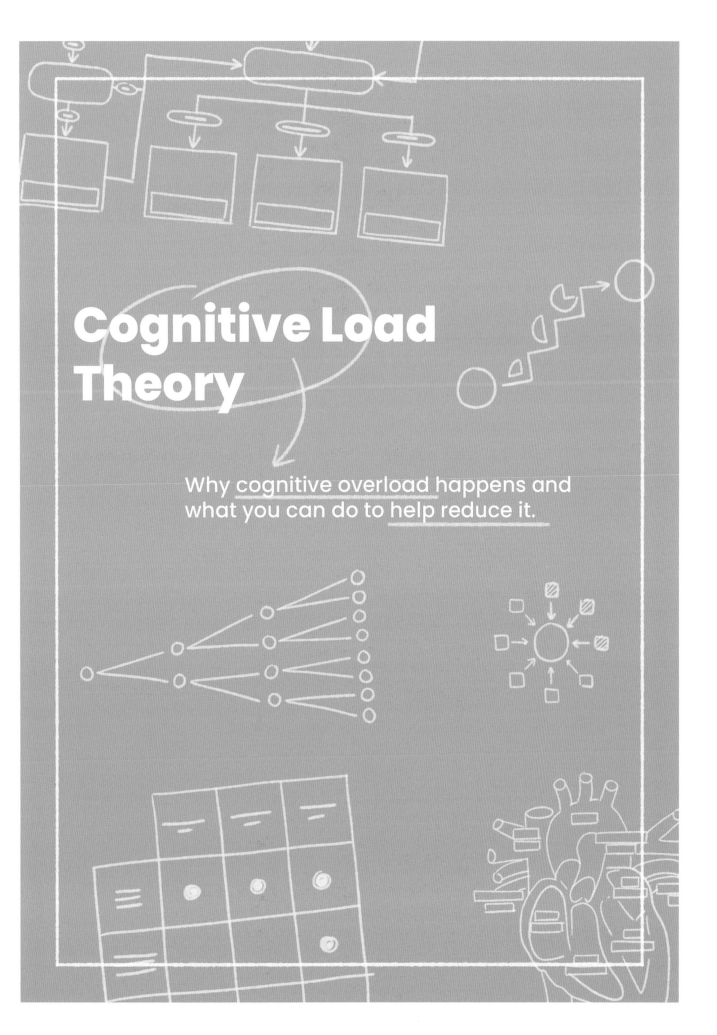

Cognitive Load Theory

Why cognitive overload happens and what you can do to help reduce it.

DOI: 10.4324/9781003334361-4

Why cognitive overload happens

Illuminated by @Inner_Drive
innerdrive.co.uk

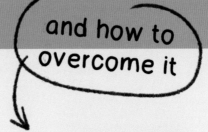

and how to overcome it

1.

The task will take too long

Break it down with shorter deadlines

2.

The task is too complex

Break it down into small chunks

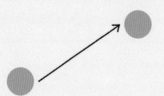

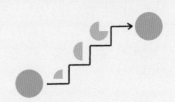

3.

There are too many choices

Highlight a clear path

4.

Too much information is presented at once

Prioritise important information

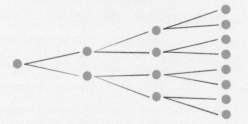

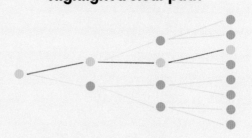

WHY COGNITIVE OVERLOAD HAPPENS

Due to the limitations and constraints of working memory, it is easy for cognitive overload to occur. When this happens, the learning process is hindered as the student is less able to transfer as much information to long-term memory.

One reason this overload occurs is that when a task will take a long time to complete, it can be difficult to picture its completion. The mental effort it takes to compute how many components and moving parts they will be required to overcome to successfully complete the task can be overwhelming. The good news is that evidence suggests that deadlines, especially those set by an external source (i.e. a teacher), can be a very effective motivator.

Likewise, when a task is complex, complicated or convoluted, it can feel nerve-racking. This can be particularly stressful for students who have a high fear of failure or have elements of perfectionism. Just as breaking the task into short deadlines can help, breaking it down into small achievable chunks will also help overcome this overload. Focusing on one part at a time can feel manageable and within their control.

Although autonomy can be a good thing, as a species we tend to struggle with too much choice. For example, one famous study found that jam sellers sold more jam when they offered only 6 different flavours, compared with when they offered 24. It seems that too much choice can be paralysing. Limiting choice and highlighting a clear path to navigate can help minimise the overload that accompanies excess choice. This is probably especially important for novice learners who have limited experiences to refer to.

Finally, too much information presented at once can lead to cognitive overload. We live in an age of abundant information. This means often the challenge isn't in seeking out more information, but in distinguishing the relevant and most important information and blocking out the redundant and irrelevant bits.

Split Attention vs Redundancy vs Coherence Effect

Illuminated by @Inner_Drive | innerdrive.co.uk

	Split-Attention Effect	Redundancy Effect	Coherence Effect
Burdens working memory	●	●	●
Information is irrelevant to the learning			●
The same information is repeated in different formats		●	
Information is split over different locations and/or timings	●		

SPLIT ATTENTION VS REDUNDANCY VS COHERENCE EFFECT

With so many different effects that relate to cognitive load theory, it is easy to be confused about the differences between them (ironically, leading to a cognitive overload about cognitive load theory). One such example is when discussing the Split Attention, Redundancy and Coherence Effects.

All three create a burden on working memory, which reduces the effectiveness of instruction, and as a result makes learning new or complex information harder. But what are the differences and distinctions between them? The Split-Attention Effect covers both relevant and new information, but is the only one that looks at physical location and/or timings. When students have to refer to two different sources of information simultaneously when learning something, this creates an extra load on their brain, as switching between multiple sources takes time, effort and energy – for example there is increased cognitive load if students have to frequently turn the page to locate integral information or have to refer to a separate key in order to understand a diagram.

Only the Coherence Effect discusses how irrelevant information competes for attention. This may include interesting but ultimately irrelevant pictures, words, music or sounds. The Redundancy Effect focuses on the repetition of the same information. For example, if asking students to read a quote, you also say it to them at the same time. This could be problematic, as people read at different speeds from the speed they hear at. This means often students read ahead of you (especially if there is a lot of text on the screen/board), leaving what you are saying as somewhat redundant.

The distinction between the three matters, as each can lead to a different strategy to help mitigate cognitive overload. Hopefully this graphic provides a handy way to distinguish between them.

Conventional vs integrated diagrams

Adapted from Jenkins, 2017 | Illuminated by @Inner_Drive | innerdrive.co.uk

Conventional

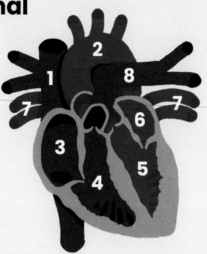

1. Vena Cava
2. Aorta
3. Right Atrium
4. Right Ventricle
5. Left Ventricle
6. Left Atrium
7. Pulmonary Veins
8. Pulmonary Artery

Integrated

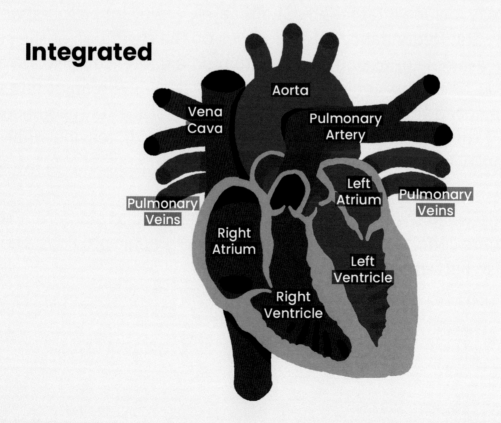

CONVENTIONAL VS INTEGRATED DIAGRAMS

The Split Attention Effect occurs when the presentation of information forces students to spread their attention too thin. This can lead to a reduced intake of important information and slow down learning, as students are unable to hold and process all the vital parts of the information.

One such example of the Split Attention Effect is how new information is presented in a diagram. Conventional diagrams typically have an image and an accompanying key. To process the information, students have to attend to both in turn. For example, in this diagram, if we asked you to describe the relationship between the Left Atrium and the Pulmonary Veins, you would have to switch between the picture of the heart and the key next to it, probably several times.

In an integrated diagram, on the other hand, the information is embedded within the picture. This means there is less switching, which makes it a less demanding process. Research has found that students take less time to process this kind of diagram and are more likely to remember the information contained within it. This means it is both more efficient and more effective.

Another unintended benefit of integrated diagrams is that we can make the image larger. Our integrated diagram of the heart is significantly larger than the conventional one, as we have freed up space by removing the text on the side. From a practical perspective, this should benefit the students who sit furthest away from the board, as it is simply easier to see it from afar.

If you need any further convincing, then think back to your time at school. Which diagram is the main one that people tend to remember? The water cycle. Which of course is probably the most famous example of an integrated diagram.

Using Cognitive Load Theory in the classroom

Illuminated by @Inner_Drive
innerdrive.co.uk

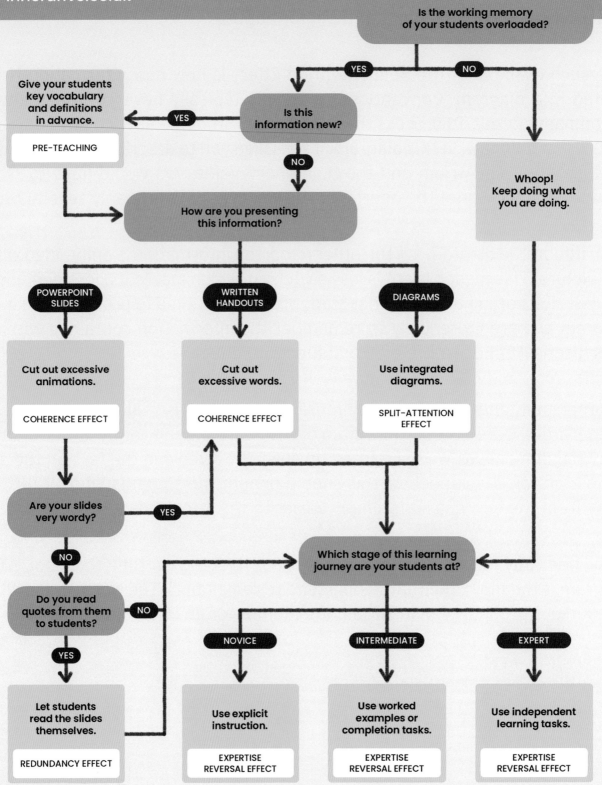

USING COGNITIVE LOAD THEORY IN THE CLASSROOM

With so many different principles that fall under the cognitive load theory umbrella, it can sometimes be confusing knowing when to apply each one (which is kind of ironic when you think about it). This flowchart is by no means intended as a set-in-stone rule, but hopefully offers a loose guide to work within.

Initially, it pays to think carefully about (a) how new the information is, and (b) the format it is delivered in. If the information is new, consider using a technique known as "Pre-teaching". This involves introducing students to key definitions beforehand. This will reduce the burden on working memory during the lesson, as they won't have to hold these key terms in their mind, and so will be able to process more information.

Where possible, consider cutting out irrelevant information. This is known as the Coherence Effect. This may take the form of reducing distracting animations in PowerPoint presentations or eliminating excessive words in written handouts. In either of these cases also consider giving ample time for students to read the material themselves. Reading quotes to them initially is probably unnecessary (assuming they can read it themselves). This is known as the Redundancy Effect.

The final principle to consider is the Expertise Reversal Effect. It states that as novices' schemas are less developed than experts', we need to teach them differently. In essence, we need to provide more of a framework for them to work within, as they don't have their own internal working model yet. Likewise, imposing our own framework on experts will compete with and confuse their own rich and nuanced schemas. So what works for one, may be detrimental to the other.

Over time, as novices become more accomplished, the support we offer should similarly fade. This is where elements such as modelling and scaffolded support become important. Given this, it is easy to see how various principles of cognitive load theory interact with some of Rosenshine's Principles.

What's Next for Cognitive Science?

What we currently know from the
research and mistakes to avoid
when applying it.

DOI: 10.4324/9781003334361-5

A beginner's guide to Cognitive Science research

Illuminated by @Inner_Drive | innerdrive.co.uk

Causation vs correlation

Causation means that X causes Y.

Correlation means that X is associated with Y.

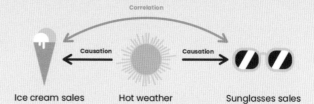

Ice cream sales   Hot weather   Sunglasses sales

Sample size

This refers to how many people took part in the study. Generally, the more participants, the more reliable the findings.

Effect size

Effect sizes, as measured by 'd', describe how significant the findings are.

The greater 'd' is, the bigger the strength of the relationship between the two variables.

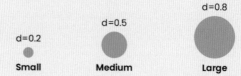

d=0.2 Small   d=0.5 Medium   d=0.8 Large

Different types of study design

Research in a laboratory

This stops or limits external factors, making it easier to determine causation of just one factor being studied.

Research in the classroom

This assesses how applicable a strategy is. It is messier as it has more external factors, but it also has more real-world validity.

Meta-analysis

This is where researchers combine a large number of similar studies to decide how impactful a strategy may be.

Longitudinal studies

These track changes in a group or individuals over a period of time, ranging from years to decades.

T I M E

Cognitive Science research is not intended to replace teacher judgement. It exists to help inform it. One study cannot give a definitive answer, but taken as part of a collection, it can help paint a picture to provide guidelines as to what might work best.

We are living in a golden of age of education embracing evidence and research. The increase in interest from teachers in cognitive science has been unprecedented over the past few years. In the quest to become even more evidence-based, more and more teachers are reading research papers and debating them.

There are no hard and fast rules as to what makes a good research paper. Sample size can be deceptive, as bigger isn't always better. Likewise effect sizes can be misleading. It can be tempting to dismiss any paper with a small effect size (in the research papers, this is about 0.2) and eulogise about high effect sizes (i.e. those above 0.8). But this is a fool's errand. A better way to think about it is the ratio of how long the intervention took compared with the effect size. For example, an effect size that is small but resulted from a cheap intervention that only took 15 minutes may be of more use than one that is larger but is complex, expensive and time-heavy.

Another important factor to consider when reading research is the issue of causality vs causation. Some research seeks to identify the cause of a behaviour or outcome, whereas others look to investigate what it is linked to. One good way to spot the latter is to pay close attention to the language researchers use. If they use phrases such as "linked to" or "associated with", there is a good chance they are not talking about "cause and effect", but about correlations.

The final consideration to reflect on is the type of research design the study uses. It is not a case of one type of design being necessarily better than another, it is more a case of seeing how well the design accurately helps us answer the research question. For example, tracking the durability and variability of change over time would suit a longitudinal study more. Likewise, wanting to get a good overview of the existing research to date would suit a meta-analysis. Each design has its strengths and weaknesses. The more you control for outside factors (i.e. with a randomised control trial), the "purer" the answer may be, though it may have less real-world implications, as things tend to be a bit messier and nuanced and complex outside of a research lab.

Cognitive Science in education

Created by Zach Groshell | Illuminated by @Inner_Drive | innerdrive.co.uk

	Modelling/Examples	Managing Cognitive Load	Dual Coding	Retrieval Practice	Spaced Practice	Interleaving	Elaborative Interrogation/Questioning	Self-explanation	Feedback
Weinstein et al, 2018	●		●	●	●	●	●	●	
Great Teaching Toolkit, 2020	●	●		●	●	●	●	●	●
Dunlosky et al, 2013				●	●	●	●	●	
Principles of Instruction, 2012	●	●		●	●		●	●	●
Cognitive Architecture and ID, 2019	●	●	●		●			●	
The Science of Learning, Deans, 2015	●	●	●	●	●	●	●	●	●
Learning: What Is It?, McCrea, 2019	●	●	●	●	●	●	●	●	●
Organizing Instruction to Improve Learning, IES, 2007	●	●	●	●	●	●	●	●	●
Cog Sci Approaches in the Classroom, EEF, 2021	●	●	●	●	●	●	●	●	●
Learning About Learning, 2016	●		●	●	●		●		●
Applying the Science of Learning in Education, 2014	●	●	●	●	●	●	●	●	●

COGNITIVE SCIENCE IN EDUCATION

Teacher Zach Groshell created and shared a version of this table on social media. It explores which elements of cognitive science are mentioned in a range of teaching and learning reviews. It is genuinely amazing to think how some of the smartest people in education, who have spent a huge amount of time and energy researching this stuff, have come to a pretty similar conclusion about our best bets for teaching and learning. It is rare, in such a diverse and complex field as education, that we achieve such a consensus.

Spaced practice, that is the act of revisiting material, appears in all reviews. It seems that it is as close as we are going to get to a universal truth that students forget things at an alarmingly fast rate and that reviewing information regularly helps cement and embed it into long-term memory. Yet despite this, students often overestimate how much they remember and therefore often feel that reviewing information is unnecessary.

Other notable mentions include retrieval practice, elaborative interrogation and self-explanation. These appear in all but one of the reviews looked at. All three, although distinct, can be grouped together, as all involve an element of recalling information from memory. This reaffirms the concept that generating an answer to a question helps students remember the information more.

The area that appears the least, though still in 8 of the 11 reviews, is dual-coding. Dual-coding is the act of combining two different types of stimuli, often pictures and words, to help students encode information more efficiently and effectively. This can be a tricky strategy to navigate, with common pitfalls including using too many pictures or ones that aren't directly related to the text that accompanies them. However, if used selectively and sparingly, it has been found to help students retain and recall more information.

Retrieval Practice

Avoid making it stressful.

Do keep it low-stakes.

Interleaving

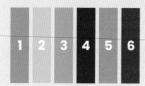

Avoid interleaving too many concepts.

Do keep it to a maximum of 3-4 concepts.

Spacing

Avoid leaving too long or too short a gap between revisiting sessions.

Do revisit material just before students forget it.

Cognitive Load Theory

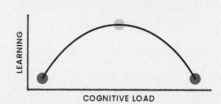

Avoid too little or too much cognitive load.

Do optimise cognitive load rather than reducing it at all costs.

Metacognition

Avoid making it vague.

Do be as clear and subject-specific as possible.

Dual Coding

Avoid using unrelated images.

Do ensure the pictures closely relate to the words and help with learning.

6 MISTAKES TO AVOID WHEN USING COGNITIVE SCIENCE

Despite its great potential to help transform education, embracing cognitive science is not without its hazards. Retrieval practice is probably the most embraced strategy within schools. And yet, if done in a high-stakes and stressful environment, it can negate some of the benefits. You can overcome this by making retrieval practice a classroom norm, as well as explaining the rationale behind doing it. We would advise against question timers and leader boards, as these can encourage students to rush their answers.

One common mistake when using interleaving is to include too many different things to interleave at once. This may be overwhelming, and students might confuse the learning material. Likewise, identifying the right time to revisit material when using spacing will be key. Leaving information too long is problematic as students' rate of forgetting is most pronounced at the beginning of their learning journey.

An easy mistake to make when focusing on cognitive load theory is to assume that less load is always better. The theory actually talks about finding an optimal load, as if it is too low, students will be bored, and if it is too high, their working memory will be overwhelmed. The Goldilocks principle of "just about right" would seem to apply well here.

Developing metacognitive skills is tricky, as evidence suggests it is best done when applied to specific subjects. This is because each subject has its own unique challenges and requirements. Vague and ambiguous advice aimed at improving metacognition is likely to be limited in impact. Finally, dual-coding, which is the act of combining information in two different forms (i.e. pictures and words), can fall short if the images aren't clearly related to the text. If this is the case, we run the risk of increasing redundant information, which can hinder the learning process.

Using cognitive science principles in the classroom can be very effective, especially when they are directly applied to learning strategies. However, as always, the devil is in the detail, and in how we implement these findings. By being aware of these common mistakes, hopefully we can use cognitive science to inform even more effective teaching and learning.

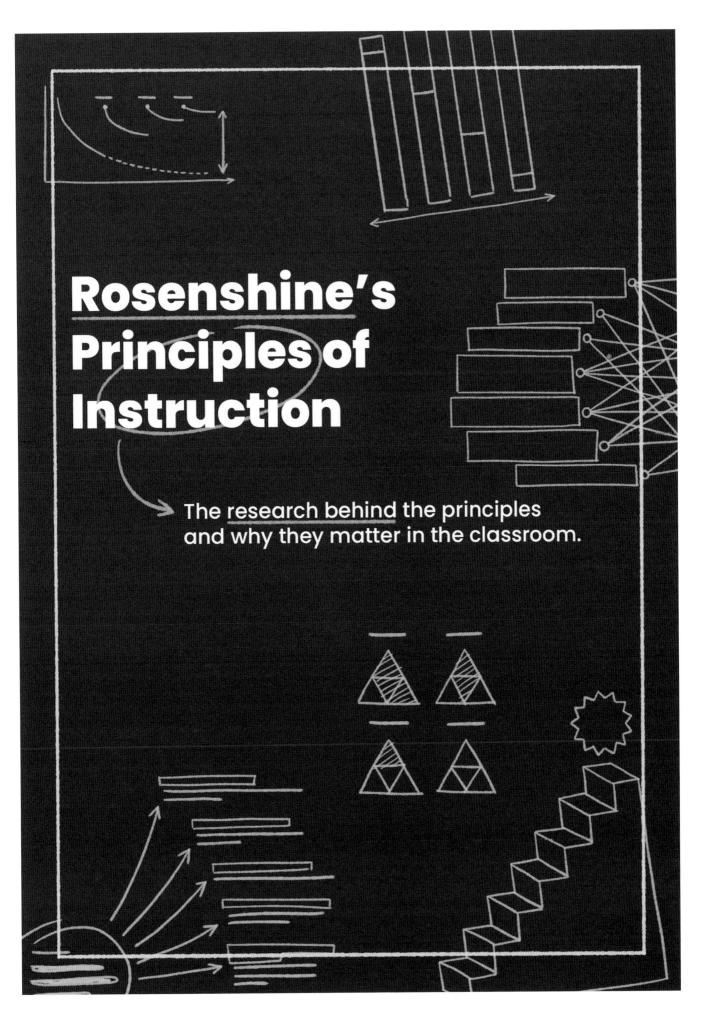

Rosenshine's Principles of Instruction

The research behind the principles and why they matter in the classroom.

DOI: 10.4324/9781003334361-6

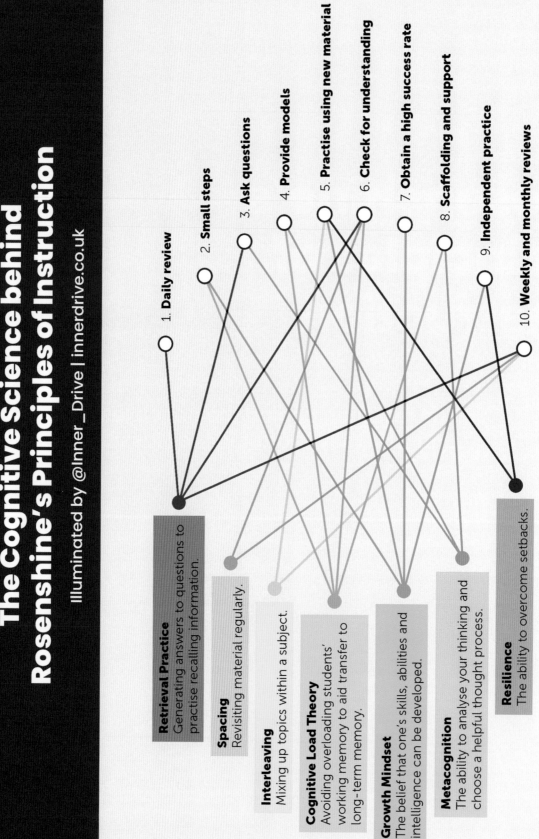

Rosenshine's Principles of Instruction have become increasingly popular in education over recent years. They offer general guidelines and suggestions as to what effective classroom teaching is grounded on. Likewise, cognitive science has also become a mainstay of education practice. This includes theories such as retrieval practice, spacing, cognitive load theory, metacognition, growth mindset and resilience. By understanding the latter, we can better apply the former.

Rosenshine's Principles were born out of studies and teaching observations. Many years later, cognitive science continues to provide a framework and explanation for why these principles may be useful. For example, if we know the research behind Retrieval Practice, then it makes sense to conduct daily review, ask questions, check for understanding and do weekly/monthly reviews. Likewise, an understanding of cognitive load theory can help us explain why taking small steps, providing models and scaffolding support are important.

Cognitive science (and indeed teaching in general) is messy. It's interlinked, complicated and often several areas overlap with one another. This is why a single intervention is unlikely to be completely effective or efficient. Often we need to consider several elements and how they combine and contribute to learning.

Both cognitive science and Rosenshine's Principles were never intended to be viewed as a checklist. It is not a case that the more elements one uses in a lesson the better. They offer a guideline or "best bet" as to what might work. Likewise, they are both intended to inform teacher judgement, and certainly not to replace it. Understanding the research that underpins the various principles can help with this.

1. **Because memories fade** – Reviews strengthen them

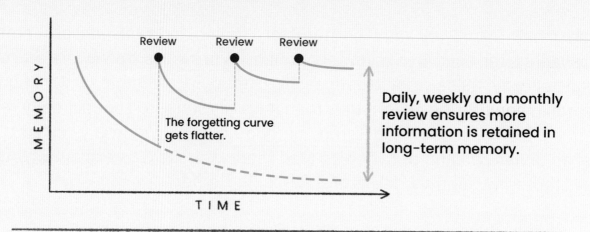

The forgetting curve gets flatter.

Daily, weekly and monthly review ensures more information is retained in long-term memory.

2. **Because misconceptions embed** – Reviews target them

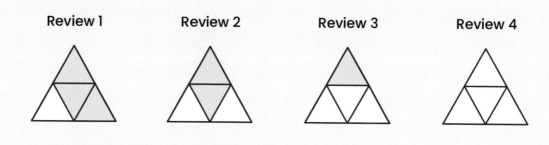

Review 1 Review 2 Review 3 Review 4

3. **Because memories change** – Reviews correct them

What you want them to remember ○ ● Faulty recollection

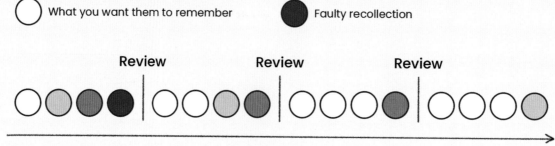

Review Review Review

TIME

WHY DAILY, WEEKLY AND MONTHLY REVIEWS MATTER

Reviewing content is so important that Rosenshine included it in two of his ten principles (principle number 1, daily review, and principle number 10, weekly and monthly review). Its importance shouldn't be underestimated, for three separate, but related, reasons.

The first is that students forget things at a much quicker rate than we would like (and faster than they often realise). Building on this, evidence suggests that regularly reviewing material helps embed information into long-term learning, which means the rate of forgetting slows down after each review. Over time, this acts as somewhat of a multiplier, resulting in a stark contrast between those who have regularly reviewed material and those who haven't.

Secondly, the act of reviewing helps us to target specific component parts, which allows us to identify where in the process students may be going wrong. This is where it is important to emphasise that Rosenshine didn't necessarily equate "review" with "quizzing". He suggests it also includes correcting homework and reviewing concepts and skills that students have used. Similarly, he also encourages teachers to ask students to identify points of difficulty, so that these can be supported and practised.

Thirdly and finally, regular reviews are important because our memories are not set in stone. They aren't akin to a file that gets stored away. They are constantly changing and being tweaked in our mind. Therefore, by reviewing the content regularly with a teacher, any faulty thinking that has begun to creep in over time can be spotted and corrected if necessary.

Sometimes reviewing previously covered material can feel like a step back. This is especially true when there is a lot of content still to cover. However, review shouldn't be thought of as a step backwards. Instead, it should be seen as a fundamental part of the learning process.

Why small steps help

Illuminated by @Inner_Drive | innerdrive.co.uk

SUCCESS

Effective
self-reflection

Easier to
fade support

Targets gaps
in knowledge

Increased
motivation

Lower
cognitive load

WHY SMALL STEPS HELP

In an age of knowledge-rich curriculums, where there is a lot of content to cover, teaching in small steps can feel slow and counterintuitive. Surely to get through more, we need to go quicker and make bigger leaps? Evidence from cognitive science suggests not, for a variety of reasons.

Due to working memory being so easy to overload, presenting too much information at once can be overwhelming and stressful. Covering new material in small incremental steps allows students to build up their schemas, which in turn, reduces the burden placed on working memory.

Likewise, by teaching using small steps, we can target specific parts of the learning journey more accurately. For example, it makes it easier to know what gaps in knowledge students have, and therefore when to fade the support we offer them. This applies to students themselves as well, as it also helps them to be more accurate when self-reflecting on their current knowledge, strengths and weaknesses.

The final benefit of small steps is that it can be very motivating for students. Previous success is one of the biggest predictors of student motivation and confidence. By making the task more complex and difficult in small steps, it helps ensure students have a deeper bank of prior achievements that they can draw on when they need to remind themselves of what they can do.

Building up skills and knowledge gradually can be time-heavy at the start – which can be frustrating. However, by ensuring that material is well learnt, and that students are motivated and confident, the learning benefits over time are considerably greater. Learning in big leaps can lead to frustrated, stressed and demotivated students who are unable to successfully link new content to their prior knowledge.

Is checking for understanding the most important of Rosenshine's Principles?

Illuminated by @Inner_Drive | innerdrive.co.uk

Rosenshine's 6th Principle

Checking for understanding helps with...

Daily Review – 1st Principle
... by ensuring there are no misconceptions in recent learning.

Small steps – 2nd Principle
... by knowing when to move on to the next level.

Ask questions – 3rd Principle
... by selecting high-quality questions.

Provide models – 4th Principle
... by choosing the best way to explain something.

Practise using new materials – 5th Principle
... by seeing how confident your students are with new information.

Obtain a high success rate – 7th Principle
... by knowing what level to pitch questions at.

Scaffold support – 8th Principle
... by enabling differentiation and personalisation of learning.

Independent practice – 9th Principle
... by knowing when your students are ready to work on their own.

Weekly and monthly review – 10th Principle
... by cementing and ingraining information into long-term memory.

One question we are often asked is "out of all of Rosenshine's Principles, which is the most important one?" After much discussion and debate, we think it is checking for understanding. This is because it is the only principle that enables all of the other nine to be implemented effectively. It is the foundation that dictates what information we present, when we present it and how we present it.

If students get the answer right when you check for understanding, it can provide a platform for them to explain and/or elaborate, which can help them make connections between the new knowledge being taught and what they already know. If they get the answer wrong, then this is also useful, as it can help us identify which areas may need to be retaught or revisited.

Checking for understanding helps with daily, weekly and monthly reviews (principles 1 and 10) because it ensures that there are no misconceptions from previous learning. This is important as it strengthens students' memory of learned information, but also ensures that they can learn new information that builds on top of previously learned knowledge.

Likewise, checking for understanding helps us know when to proceed to the next step of the learning principle. This is a cornerstone of teaching using small steps (principle 2), obtaining a high success rate (principle 7) and scaffolding support (principle 8).

One principle that is completely entwined with the concept of checking for understanding is principle number 3, asking questions. Questions in the classroom serve multiple purposes; they increase curiosity, focus attention and can increase the rate of learning. But underpinning all of that is that they allow us to check for understanding.

By regularly checking students' understanding, teachers can not only get a better view of what their students know, but how much they know and how well they know it. This is why it is arguably Rosenshine's most important principle.

Scaffolding support and providing models

Illuminated by @Inner _Drive | innerdrive.co.uk

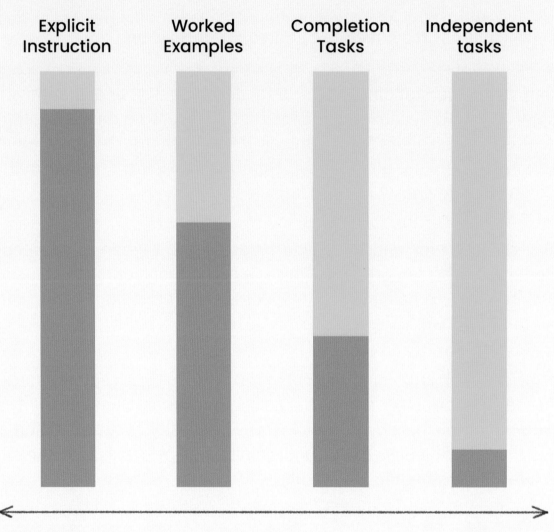

The teacher provides the framework

The student does the problem solving

Explicit Instruction

Worked Examples

Completion Tasks

Independent tasks

Novices

Experts

SCAFFOLDING SUPPORT AND PROVIDING MODELS

How we give instructions and information to students when they are learning new or complex information plays a key role in their learning. This covers several of Rosenshine's Principles, from providing models, to scaffolding support, to teaching using small steps.

Explicit Instruction is when a teacher gives clear, specific instructions to students on how to complete a task or an assignment. Research suggests that giving students explicit instructions is a very effective teaching strategy, especially for novice learners.

The Expertise Reversal Effect, which falls under the umbrella of cognitive load theory, is based on the idea that novices do not learn the same way that experts do. For novices, learning new information can be highly intimidating and sometimes overwhelming, as they do not have their own highly developed schemas to rely on. On the other hand, experts have schema-based knowledge, which guides them through tasks with less need for external support. If they are given explicit instruction on top of this, there will be an overlap of information between the expert's own personal schemas and experiences and the explicit instruction. This means additional working memory resources will be required to decipher the best information to use, which may result in cognitive overload and slow down the learning process.

As students develop their knowledge, and as such are at a stage between novice and expert, they may benefit from worked examples and completion tasks. With worked examples, a step-by-step process is provided for them to follow. This helps them to start to internalise the processes they need to follow. Likewise, completion tasks, which get progressively more difficult, help fade the support we offer in tandem with their developing knowledge and skills.

Quite counterintuitively, this all means that the best way to develop expert independent learners isn't to give students more independent tasks from the start. Instead, it may be better to initially give them very explicit instruction, and then over time gradually fade the support as their expertise develops.

Success and high expectations

Illuminated by @Inner_Drive | innerdrive.co.uk

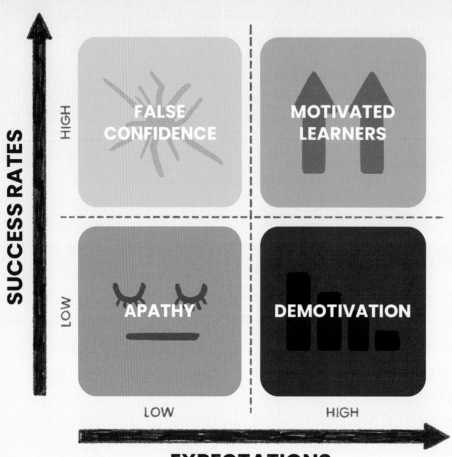

SUCCESS RATES (vertical axis: LOW → HIGH)

- FALSE CONFIDENCE
- MOTIVATED LEARNERS
- APATHY
- DEMOTIVATION

EXPECTATIONS (horizontal axis: LOW → HIGH)

False confidence
Only succeeding in easy tasks feels good in the short term, but leads to brittle confidence.

Motivated learners
The sweet spot of motivation comes from experiencing success in ambitious environments.

Apathy
When a lack of success is combined with a lackadaisical setting, it quickly leads to indifference.

Demotivation
Consistently failing when everyone expects you to do better is frustrating and demoralising.

SUCCESS AND HIGH EXPECTATIONS

Sometimes psychological research throws up contradictions. Two different areas, taken in isolation, provide strategies that can help inform teacher practice. And yet, when viewed together, they appear to contradict each other. Balancing high expectations and achieving high success rates is one such example.

There is a wealth of evidence that highlights how if teachers have high expectations of their students, these students tend to perform better. This is known as the Pygmalion Effect (so named after a sculptor in Greek mythology who had such high expectations for his statue, it turned into a real person). High expectations have a positive impact as students take their cue from their teachers, internalising their teachers' high beliefs, and also they lead to teachers asking their students more challenging questions.

Separately, research has suggested that in order to aid learning and motivation, we want students to achieve a high level of success before moving on to the next task. For example, one research review found that an optimal success rate, in terms of learning, on a multiple-choice test is around 75%. Barak Rosenshine suggested something similar as one of his principles. This naturally lends itself to starting students on small easier tasks which will help them achieve success, before increasing the level of difficulty as their skills progress.

However, it can be tricky to maintain high expectations whilst also striving to achieve a high success rate, as the latter can easily morph and mutate into "dumbing down" and creating a culture of low expectations. This is known as the Golem Effect and has a negative effect on student achievement.

So how can you maintain high expectations whilst achieving high success rates? We think the key is to ensure the culture of high expectations means not just focusing on outcomes, but focusing more on behaviours and attitudes. Measuring success against individual development, instead of comparing with others, will also help with this.

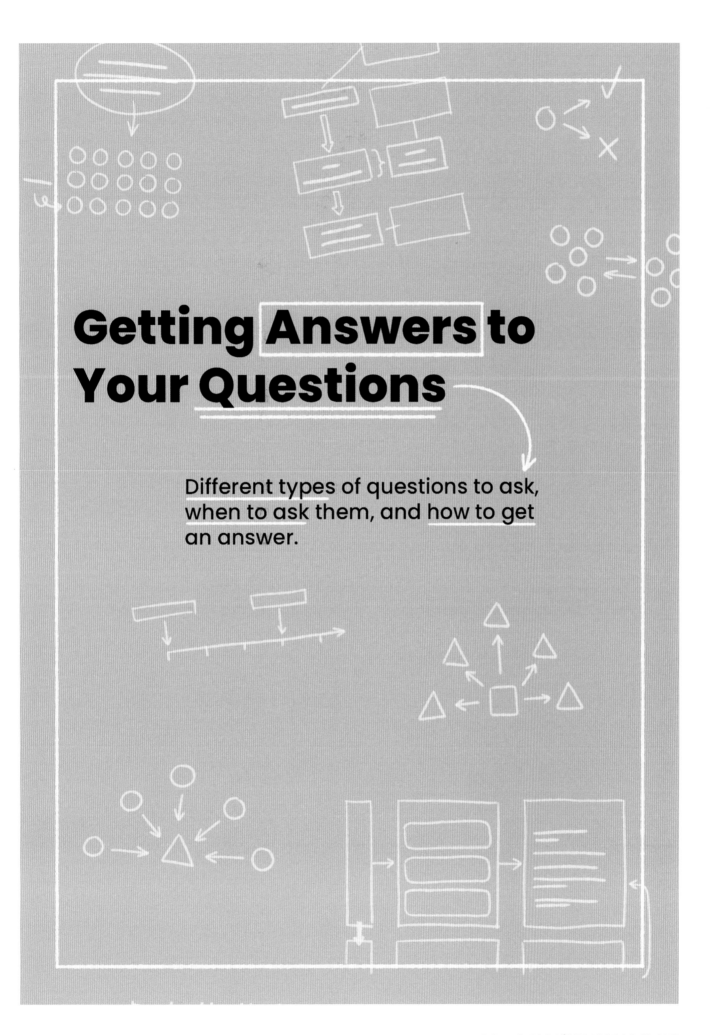

Getting Answers to Your Questions

Different types of questions to ask, when to ask them, and how to get an answer.

DOI: 10.4324/9781003334361-7

Questions to check for knowledge and understanding

Adapted from Lieban, 2019 | Illuminated by @Inner_Drive | innerdrive.co.uk

Factual Questions

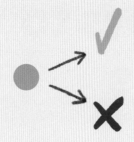

"What date was the
Battle of Hastings?"

Convergent Questions

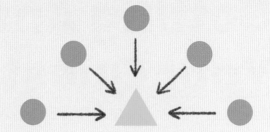

"Why did William the
Conqueror invade England?"

Divergent Questions

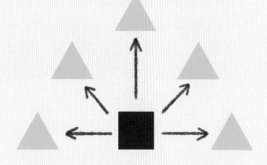

"What would have happened
if William the Conqueror
had not invaded England?"

Evaluative Questions

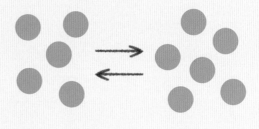

"What are the similarities and
differences between William's
and Caesar's invasions?"

QUESTIONS TO CHECK FOR KNOWLEDGE AND UNDERSTANDING

Asking the right question at the right time can help improve knowledge and check for understanding. Factual questions are questions that have a definitive right or wrong answer, such as "when was the Battle of Hastings?" They take little time to both ask and answer. They can be used to build up a student's core knowledge and so are probably best used at the beginning of a learner's journey into a topic.

Convergent questions are ones that may have several "correct" answers that lie within a commonly accepted range. An example would be "Why did William the Conqueror invade England?" The student has to work harder to answer it. These questions help develop broader knowledge and can help add context and nuance to a student's understanding.

At a higher level of cognitive thinking we have divergent questions. These are similar to hypothetical "what if" questions. There are technically no correct answers, as the question is more concerned with how students use their knowledge base, imagination and analysis. An example of this would be "What would have happened if William the Conqueror had not invaded England?" Divergent questions may take longer to answer and can lead the discussion down unexpected avenues. This means they are associated with conceding both time and control.

Evaluative questions are compare-and-contrast questions. An example would be "What are the similarities and differences between William's and Caesar's invasions of Britain?" To be answered well, students need factual knowledge from a number of different areas. This is another type of questioning that requires a higher level of cognitive thinking and can be a prompt for deep and layered retrieval practice.

It is worth emphasising that it is not suggested that some types of questions are better than others. It is about asking the right question at the right time. As well as effectiveness, factors like base knowledge, available time and control over the direction of the conversation all need to be considered.

Using psychologically rich questions in the classroom

Illuminated by @Inner_Drive | innerdrive.co.uk

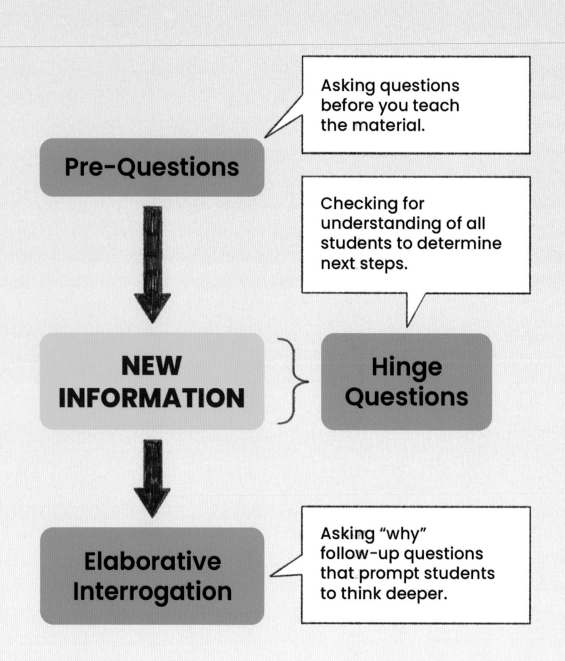

USING PSYCHOLOGICALLY RICH QUESTIONS IN THE CLASSROOM

Asking the right question, at the right time, has the capacity to target specific elements of knowledge, as well as giving an indication of students' thought processes. Questions can serve different purposes, from increasing curiosity, to checking understanding, to linking with previously taught content.

Pre-Questions are an example of asking questions to capture attention and increase interest. This is when you ask a question before teaching the content. So, for example, asking "how many fish do you think there are in the Atlantic Ocean?" before covering that information later on. Evidence suggests that these type of questions lead to an increase in learning, as when you come to that part of the lesson, students have already been primed that it is important information, and pay more attention as a result.

Hinge Questions are typically asked at the midpoint of a lesson, with the intention of gauging how much of the content students have understood so far. Their answers then help the teacher decide how to proceed with the next part of the lesson. Ideally, these are simple quick questions that require all students to answer.

Elaborative Interrogation is asking questions after you teach the content, with the specific purpose of helping students link the current content with what they already know. It helps them by making connections, which not only consolidates the existing information, but also helps develop a richer and more nuanced schema. One such example of Elaborative Interrogation would be "why would this be true for X and not for Y?" In order to answer this type of question, they have to retrieve everything they know about X, everything they know about Y, and think hard about the similarities and differences. Doing this helps students cement the information in their long-term memory.

How to create a warm environment to cold-call in

Illuminated by @Inner_Drive | innerdrive.co.uk

Provide the rationale

Explain why you use cold-calling.

START HERE

Do it early

This sets the norms of participation.

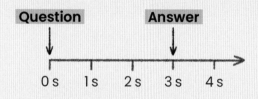

Increase wait times

This increases thinking time and helps students not feel unprepared.

Use Think, Pair, Share

This helps students get comfortable with sharing an answer.

Frame errors helpfully

This reduces the fear of failure and the taboo of getting it wrong.

Use positive body language

This helps students feel listened to and respected.

HOW TO CREATE A WARM ENVIRONMENT TO COLD-CALL IN

Lately there has been a renewed interest and popularity amongst teachers for using a questioning method known as 'cold-calling'. Cold-calling refers to any activity where a teacher solicits an answer from a student regardless of whether they have raised their hand or not. Its popularity can be linked to the growing evidence supporting the benefit of retrieval practice, as cold-calling can help ensure all students attempt to retrieve the information.

Some may worry that cold-calling can lead to students feeling 'picked on', potentially resulting in them feeling embarrassed or victimised if they do not know the answer. However, research has found that the more students participate in classes with high cold-calling rates, the more comfortable they feel and the less fear they have about speaking in class.

For cold-calling to be effective, it has to be done in a warm way. Evidence suggests that providing a clear explanation of why it is being done and doing it early can help create an expectation of participation.

For it to be effective, teachers need to give students ample opportunity to reflect and respond to the question. This is where factors such as wait times, which is the gap left between asking a question and asking for an answer, become important. Likewise, activities such as 'Think-Pair-Share' can help. This is where students get some personal thinking time, before telling the person next to them their answer, before then sharing it with the rest of the class.

How should teachers deal with incorrect answers during cold-calling? There is a fine line to be trodden between the dangers of demotivating students who get the answer wrong and patronising them with false praise. Strategies to help include: framing errors helpfully by highlighting what aspects were correct, asking other students to elaborate on the initial answer, as well as using open and positive body language.

The power of cold-calling & wait times

Created by Doug Lemov & Luke Taylor
Illuminated by @Inner_Drive | innerdrive.co.uk

Who is doing Retrieval Practice in the class?

Laura*, what's the capital of Australia?

Just Laura

Laura*

What's the capital of Australia, Laura*?

The quickest in the class | Just Laura

What's the capital of Australia.................................Laura*?

The quickest in the class | Everyone in the class | Just Laura

* Other names are available

THE POWER OF COLD-CALLING & WAIT TIMES

Under the right conditions (i.e. low stakes), generating an answer to a question can help accelerate student learning. It is therefore very important that we reflect on how we can best frame and structure these questions.

But what makes a good cold-calling question? The subtle but important difference in the three approaches depicted in the graphic has a significant impact on how much learning the whole class does. If we tell students at the start of the question who we want an answer from, we subconsciously give the rest of the class permission to switch off, as they know they are not going to be asked for an answer. As a result, they don't have to recall the information and so miss out on the benefit of retrieval practice. In fact, it is likely that only Laura will get the benefit.

By contrast, if we use Laura's name at the end of the question, we increase the amount of time the rest of the class are being asked to recall the answer. Despite the fact that they are subsequently not chosen, they have still engaged in this retrieval practice. This means both Laura and the rest of the class are reflecting on the task for longer.

Cold-calling is one of many strategies that teachers can employ as part of their practice when it comes to asking questions. It has its merits, but is by no means the only way to frame a question. There is a time and place for it. Arguably, it is not as effective if students are novices with little baseline knowledge. This is because it only allows the teacher to check the understanding of one student at a time, and so potentially isn't best used if there is a chance of misconceptions being left undiscovered in others.

Teacher wait times vs other really fast things

Illuminated by @Inner_Drive | innerdrive.co.uk

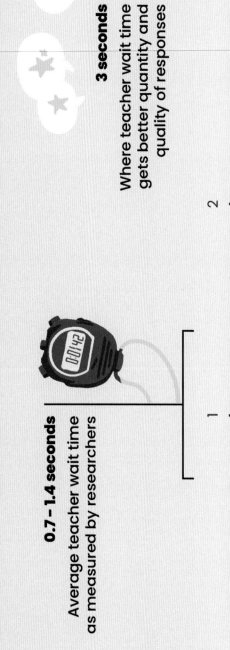

0.7 – 1.4 seconds
Average teacher wait time as measured by researchers

3 seconds
Where teacher wait time gets better quantity and quality of responses

0.8 seconds
One heartbeat at average resting rate

1.8 seconds
The fastest F1 pit stop ever

0.3 seconds
The time it takes to blink

0.165 seconds
An elite sprinter's reaction time

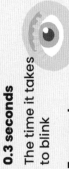

TEACHER WAIT TIMES VS OTHER REALLY FAST THINGS

How long a teacher waits after asking a question before they solicit an answer from a student is known as their 'wait time'. A good wait time allows the students to engage in deeper retrieval, which can lead to greater learning gains. Unfortunately, there is no clear-cut answer as to how long an optimal wait time is, as it depends on too many factors, such as the type of question, how much your students already know and what the purpose of the question is.

Whilst we don't know the ideal length, we can suggest the cost of rushing wait times. This includes students feeling demotivated and giving up, an increase in sloppy mistakes and students guessing the answer with little thought. The latter is especially problematic, as if they get it right and you don't know whether it was because they really knew it or they just got lucky, it is difficult to know whether to re-teach it or move on.

Some research papers have found that the average time a teacher waits is between 0.7 and 1.4 seconds. Given that this is a bit more than a heartbeat and a bit less than an F1 pit stop, it is likely that under these conditions, students are just giving their first answer, not necessarily their best one.

One study did examine what happens if you wait at least three seconds. The researchers found that both the quantity and quality of answers increased, as well as a reduction of "I don't know" answers. This is not to say that 2.9 seconds is bad and 3.1 seconds is good, but just that it is worth considering how much time is enough to improve the response rate whilst not demotivating the quickest in class. Sometimes the time we wait can feel prolonged and awkward, but potentially, this is where better learning happens.

How to Think, Pair, Share

Created by Jamie Clark | Illuminated by @Inner_Drive | innerdrive.co.uk

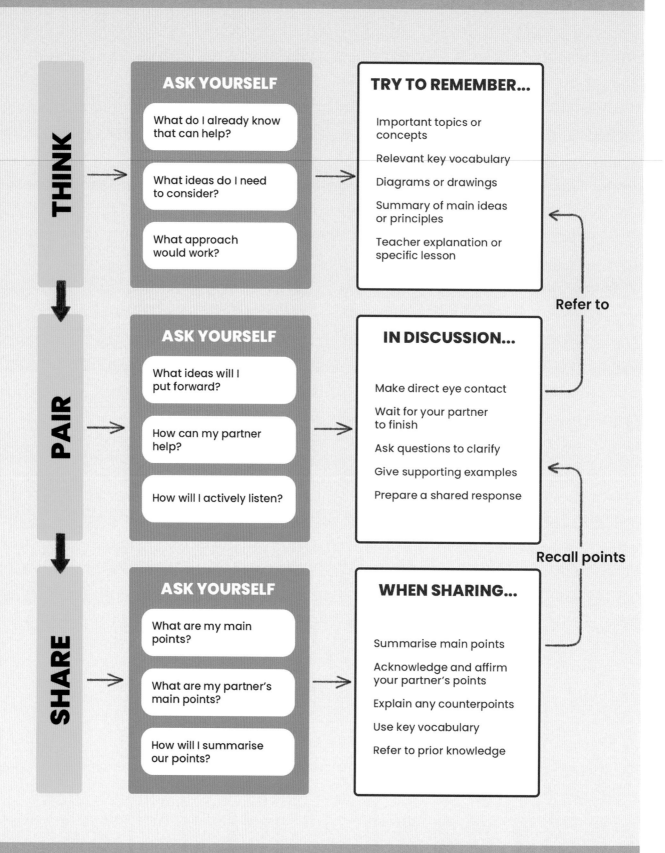

THINK

ASK YOURSELF

- What do I already know that can help?
- What ideas do I need to consider?
- What approach would work?

TRY TO REMEMBER...

- Important topics or concepts
- Relevant key vocabulary
- Diagrams or drawings
- Summary of main ideas or principles
- Teacher explanation or specific lesson

Refer to

PAIR

ASK YOURSELF

- What ideas will I put forward?
- How can my partner help?
- How will I actively listen?

IN DISCUSSION...

- Make direct eye contact
- Wait for your partner to finish
- Ask questions to clarify
- Give supporting examples
- Prepare a shared response

Recall points

SHARE

ASK YOURSELF

- What are my main points?
- What are my partner's main points?
- How will I summarise our points?

WHEN SHARING...

- Summarise main points
- Acknowledge and affirm your partner's points
- Explain any counterpoints
- Use key vocabulary
- Refer to prior knowledge

HOW TO THINK, PAIR, SHARE

'Think-Pair-Share' is a technique that has become increasingly popular in recent years. This is because it can be a very effective way to help students better engage in deep retrieval practice, as well as increasing their ability to communicate and participate in classroom discussions with their peers.

The 'Think' part is where the vast majority of retrieval takes place. If we want students to effectively engage in this process, we have to allow them sufficient time here. This means giving them time to consider their best answer, not just their first one. This can be done by getting them to ask themselves metacognitive questions that link the new content with previously learnt material.

The 'Pair' stage serves three key purposes. First, by having students explain their thoughts to a peer, it prompts them to clarify and organise their ideas. Second, it can help students develop their answers as they learn from one another. Third and finally, it can help reduce any nerves about sharing their ideas with the whole class, by initially doing so with just one partner.

Finally, we arrive at the 'Share' stage. This entails students summarising the main points and articulating them to the rest of the class. Doing so in their own words allows for a deep processing and shows authentic learning. This helps the teacher check for understanding, and offers opportunities to follow up on any misconceptions and to emphasise any correct key points that have been raised.

'Think-Pair-Share' is one of many strategies that can help students engage with the questions we ask them. Monitoring for any misconceptions before they spread, and leaving a good amount of time for each phase, allows for the dual win of both retrieval practice and oracy skills.

Feedback

When and how to use feedback
to support your students' learning
and progress.

DOI: 10.4324/9781003334361-8

The 4 types of feedback (and their consequences)

Illuminated by @Inner _Drive | innerdrive.co.uk

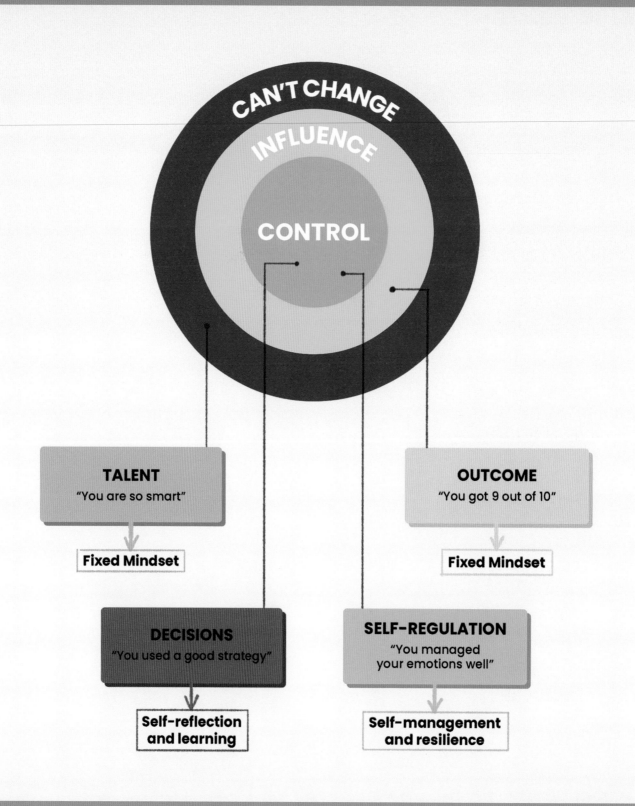

THE 4 TYPES OF FEEDBACK (AND THEIR CONSEQUENCES)

Giving feedback can be a double-edged sword. If it is done right, it can be one of the most effective ways to help someone improve their learning. Many researchers have found that constructive feedback is an incredibly powerful tool for promoting children's social, moral and intellectual development.

However, other research demonstrated that 38% of feedback interventions do more harm than good. That is to say that those students would have done better if they had been left alone rather than been given any feedback. Sometimes, what we intend to be encouraging and helpful can easily be interpreted as judgemental and critical. It's therefore important to get our feedback right.

In terms of giving feedback, it is helpful to know that researchers have identified four different types of feedback that one could give. It is not a case of one necessarily being better than the others, but rather matching the type of feedback to the specific context. The four different types of feedback relate to the person, the outcome of the task, the process and their self-regulation.

Feedback on the person ("you are so smart") is risky, as although in the short term it may make students feel good, in the long term it may not lead to much learning, as it doesn't tell the student what they could improve on. For many, that is seen as something that they cannot change.

Feedback on the outcome of the task is often effective if students had a faulty interpretation of what they needed to do. Feedback on the process, which is about the strategy and decisions they made to complete the task, often leads to deep learning as it can act as a prompt to seek out more information. This is because it is something they can actively control themselves next time.

Finally, feedback about self-regulation, which is something else the learner has a degree of control over, is often effective for novice learners.

3 key feedback questions to ask

Illuminated by @Inner_Drive | innerdrive.co.uk

1. "Where am I going?"

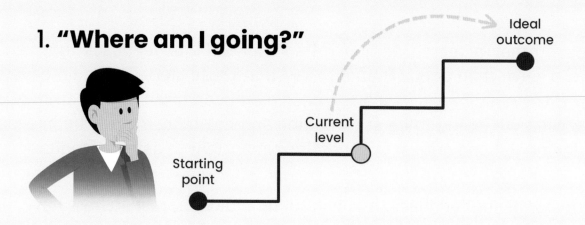

2. "How am I going?"

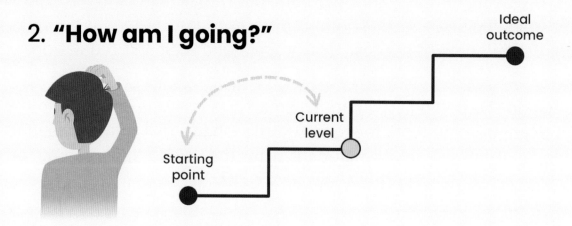

3. "Where to next?"

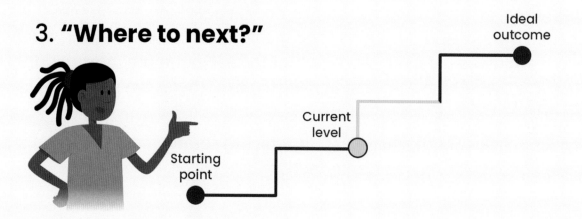

Reference: Hattie & Timperley, 2007

3 KEY FEEDBACK QUESTIONS TO ASK

Psychologist and Nobel Prize winner Daniel Kahneman once commented that "true intuitive expertise is learned from prolonged experience with good feedback on mistakes". All too often, the onus of feedback is with the giver, not the receiver. But for it to be most useful, the receiver must be proactive in seeking out the feedback. This means learning how to ask good questions themselves.

Researchers Helen Timperley and John Hattie published one of our favourite studies on feedback. Part of it included three great questions that should be asked (and answered) in order to learn from feedback. These are "Where am I going?", "How am I going?" and "Where to next?"

"Where am I going?" is a powerful question as it starts with the end in mind. This can help provide clarity and focus on what students are working towards. It also increases motivation, akin to a light at the end of the tunnel, which can be important during times of struggle and setbacks.

"How am I going?" helps students monitor and measure their progress. As this is self-referenced (i.e. measured against their own previous performance), it is a contributing factor to areas such as resilience, self-regulation and grit.

"Where to next?" provides concrete and actionable steps for moving forward. It reduces ambiguity, doubt and confusion. Knowing specific steps to work on can be incredibly motivating and also provides accountability for future conversations.

These three questions aren't intended to be an exhaustive list of feedback questions. Instead, they act as a baseline and a prompt for further conversations. They are initial starters that can get the ball rolling on discussion about self-improvement and development.

When to give feedback

Illuminated by @Inner_Drive | innerdrive.co.uk

Are you telling students whether they got an answer right or wrong, or providing an overall summary of their performance and how they can improve?

RIGHT / WRONG

SUMMARISING PERFORMANCE

Is the student likely to have a negative emotional reaction to the feedback?

Are you aiming to motivate students to continue with a task, or to achieve deeper understanding of the material and enhance memory?

YES

NO

MOTIVATE

DEEP UNDERSTANDING

Give feedback very quickly.

Give feedback within an immediate timeframe but after a small delay, for example at the end of the lesson.

Provide feedback on the same day.

Is the feedback simple and possible to process automatically, or is it complex and requiring effortful processing?

SIMPLE

COMPLEX

Provide feedback within a delayed timeframe, from the next day to a week later.

WHEN TO GIVE FEEDBACK

The debate over whether immediate or delayed feedback is better has become muddied by the highly inconsistent definitions of what immediate and delayed feedback actually are. With the lack of a definitive timescale for each type of feedback, it's no wonder that there are conflicting views out there on which is better.

Unfortunately no clear or simple answer exists as to which is better. As with most research (and indeed teaching and learning), the answer is filled with nuances, caveats and asterisks. This is because immediate and delayed feedback can serve different purposes.

We can broadly classify feedback into two types: corrective and evaluative. Corrective feedback is where we inform a student of whether they got an answer right or not. Evaluative feedback provides comments about how well the students did and what they could have done better. It is generally felt that corrective feedback is best delivered quickly, so as to help students stay on task and not let any misconceptions take root. Evaluative feedback typically involves more reflection, and can be delivered once the dust has started to settle.

One other factor to consider is the length of the task a student is being given feedback on. The longer the task, the more beneficial it may be to delay feedback. This is because shorter tasks are likely to prompt feedback that is easy to process automatically, while longer tasks are likely to need more detailed feedback which will require effortful processing.

One final thing to consider is that a student's personality will affect how well they receive feedback at different times. Some students may react negatively to immediate feedback – as they can get frustrated, upset or defensive when corrected for an incorrect answer. In these cases, it may be better to approach these students after a small delay, so that they can reflect upon and process feedback in a calmer state.

THE FOUR PET HATES OF THE BRAIN

Why is it that some students argue about the feedback they get given, whereas others are more likely to take it on board and action it? The answer could be, in part, because one or more of the pet hates of the brain have been triggered. Given that a wealth of research has found that effective feedback is one of the biggest accelerators of student learning, it is a question worth deeply considering.

The four pet hates of the brain are unfairness, uncertainty, a lack of control and reduced status. If students misinterpret the feedback we give them as representing one of these pet hates, they are likely to respond in a defensive, dismissive and/or argumentative way. The four pet hates are drawn from Dr David Rock's SCARF model, but individually have been supported by research on the fear of failure, thinking biases and emotional regulation. Other pet hates that set emotional alarm bells ringing likely exist, but these four offer a firm foundation to start with.

Key to having feedback accepted is understanding which of the four pet hates is most prominent for each of your students. For example, if students have a strong sense of fairness, then feedback that is seen as inconsistent with previous reactions will be distressing. Likewise, if they have a strong desire for certainty or control, then predictability is key. If they are driven by status, then any feedback that is perceived to be negative that is delivered in public is more likely to be rejected.

These pet hates explain why two different students react very differently to the same sort of feedback. This is one of the reasons why positive teacher–student relationships are important, as the better you know your students, the easier it is to adjust and adapt accordingly.

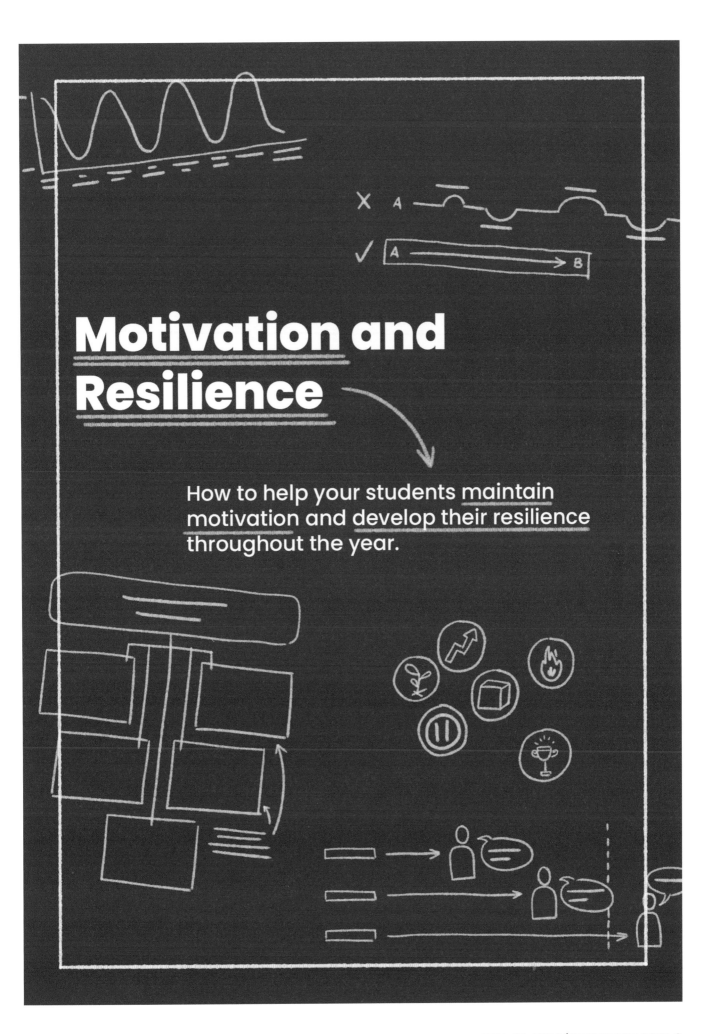

Motivation and Resilience

How to help your students maintain motivation and develop their resilience throughout the year.

DOI: 10.4324/9781003334361-9

Creating resilient environments

Illuminated by @Inner_Drive | innerdrive.co.uk

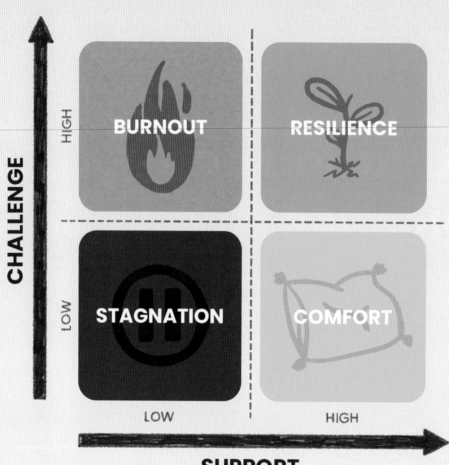

CHALLENGE

HIGH — BURNOUT | RESILIENCE

LOW — STAGNATION | COMFORT

LOW | HIGH

SUPPORT

Burnout
Lots of stress and frustration. This is unsustainable and leads to burnout.

Resilience
If students are both challenged and supported, resilience can develop and thrive.

Stagnation
Not much happens here. Students are likely to, at best, plateau.

Comfort
This is nice, but ultimately, high performance doesn't tend to happen here.

Reference: Fletcher and Sarkar, 2016

CREATING RESILIENT ENVIRONMENTS

The word "resilience" in education is in danger of becoming the number one buzzword. Resilience has been used to cover a whole range of behaviours and areas, from well-being, to coping with exam pressure, to independent learning. It has spawned many posters, assemblies and PHSE lessons. And yet, the research behind it is often less well known.

In arguably the most important research paper on the topic, researchers explored what factors contribute to helping create a resilient environment. They whittled it down to just two: challenge and support. The level of challenge refers to how demanding the task or setting is. And the level of support covers how supported students feel they are.

If we create an environment that is low in challenge and low in support, things stagnate. Not much happens there. The top left box is a particularly interesting box, as if we raise the level of challenge but don't increase the level of support, people tend to experience stress, anxiety and eventually burnout. It is relentless and unsustainable.

If we create an environment that is low in challenge but is very supportive, then that is really comfortable. It is nice, it is reassuring, it feels safe, but we do have to acknowledge that high performance is unlikely to happen there.

The evidence suggests that in order to create an environment where resilience can flourish, we need to set the level of challenge high, but to also complement that with high levels of support. This will help ensure that students are striving to improve and experiencing a good level of desirable difficulty, whilst also feeling psychologically safe enough to fail, as they know they will be supported.

Developing resilience is very difficult. It is more than a cheesy slogan or a case of just "believing in yourself". It is rooted in culture. If the ethos is underpinned by high challenge and high support, then we give our students the best chance of improving this key trait.

What is fear of failure?

Illuminated by @Inner_Drive | innerdrive.co.uk

Fear of failure is the fear of...

Shame and embarrassment

Research suggests this is the most pronounced fear

Important others losing interest

The belief that we're more valuable and interesting if we succeed

Devaluing one's self-estimate

A fancy way of saying having to lower your opinion of yourself

Upsetting important others

This is the worry that we'll let people down by failing

Having an uncertain future

i.e., "If I do badly in exams, I don't know what university I'll go to"

These both typically relate to parents, teachers, other family members or friends

Reference: Conroy et al, 2001

WHAT IS FEAR OF FAILURE?

It is often not failure itself that students fear. It is the perceived negative consequences that follow from that failure that stress them out. This has been increasingly studied in business, sport and education. Anecdotally, it feels like it is a growing issue for many students.

Numerous studies have found that high levels of fear of failure can lead to lower self-esteem, avoiding challenging tasks, being pessimistic and even cheating. It has also been associated with perfectionism and poor coping strategies, such as ignoring the problem in the misguided hope it will simply disappear. There are five main components that contribute to one's level of fear of failure. These five components are: experiencing shame and embarrassment, being forced to readjust how you see yourself, worries about an uncertain future, upsetting important others and important others losing interest.

A number of research studies have found that the fear of failure that is consistently the highest is fear of shame and embarrassment. This makes sense, as by definition we are social creatures. No one wants to be laughed at or embarrassed by their failures. This is why failure in private often has very different and lower emotional resonance than failure experienced in public. Given that we also know from a wealth of research that teenagers feel social rejection more acutely, as well as placing a higher value on social status, it is not surprising that for many the fear of shame and embarrassment is the highest.

A fear of shame and embarrassment is seen in students who don't volunteer an answer to a question due to a fear of being teased if they get it wrong. For these people, they can quickly internalise the belief that trying hard isn't cool. With a high fear of failure, trying and failing definitely isn't. We can help them overcome this by being vigilant against any form of behaviour that is done to mock others following a failure, even and especially if it is done under the guise of "banter".

How to overcome procrastination

Illuminated by @Inner_Drive | innerdrive.co.uk

75% of students consider themselves procrastinators

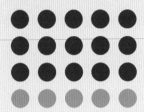

The characteristics of procrastinators:

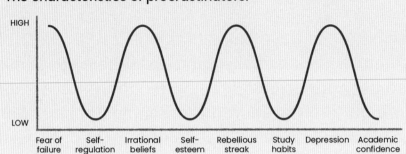

Fear of failure	Self-regulation	Irrational beliefs	Self-esteem	Rebellious streak	Study habits	Depression	Academic confidence

Strategies to overcome procrastination

1. Block out potential distractions

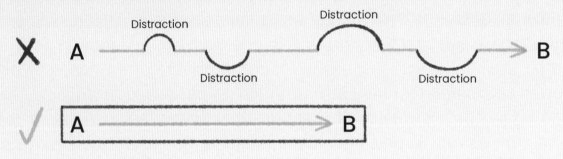

2. Leave plenty of time

This gap is known as the Planning Fallacy

How long students think a task will take

How long a task actually takes

3. Just start the task

Starting a task is the hardest part, but also the most important

The Zeigarnik Effect kicks in to help you complete the task

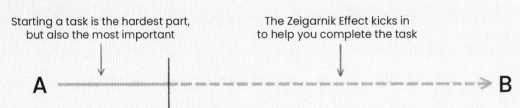

HOW TO OVERCOME PROCRASTINATION

William James, who is often referred to as the "Father of American Psychology", once stated that "nothing is so fatiguing as the eternal hanging on of an uncompleted task". This is a cause for concern when taken in combination with research that suggests 75% of students consider themselves procrastinators.

There is no singular reason why students procrastinate. Evidence suggests that it is most common in those with low self-esteem, low academic confidence and low self-regulation and those with high fear of failure, depression or rebellious streaks. In the short term, procrastination may provide a benefit, in that it helps them avoid the prospect of failing at a task (i.e. you can't fail at it if you don't do it), but long term this self-handicapping behaviour makes the thing they are most worried about more likely to occur.

Just as there is no singular cause, there is also no singular strategy for overcoming it. Minimising distractions probably provides an easier route compared with trying to enhance self-control. If the distractions are out of sight, students are less likely to procrastinate.

The Planning Fallacy, which states that people often underestimate how long a task will take to complete, can lead to procrastination. Evidence suggests that getting students to reflect on previous similar tasks they have done in the past, along with predicting the obstacles they may face when trying to complete a task, may help make their time predictions more accurate.

Likewise, simply starting a task may be half the battle, with the momentum generated helping drive positive behaviours. The Zeigarnik Effect describes how once a task has been started, it creates a type of cognitive tension that exists until it is completed. This means students should be encouraged to begin, as this can improve both memory and motivation.

The benefits of knowing multiple strategies

Illuminated by @Inner_Drive | innerdrive.co.uk

SUCCESS

**When students know
only one strategy**

Strategy X

I'm not good
at this subject

**When students know
multiple strategies**

Strategy X

I'll try another
strategy

Strategy Y

I'll try another
strategy

Strategy Z

I did it!

THE BENEFITS OF KNOWING MULTIPLE STRATEGIES

Teaching students multiple strategies can help them develop their motivation, resilience and self-regulation. If students only know one way to solve a problem, then if/when that method doesn't work, there is a chance that they will confuse the efficacy of that strategy with their ability and aptitude for that subject. This can lead to students putting themselves in self-limiting boxes, believing things such as "I'm not a maths person".

Doing so can lead to a state of what psychologists call "learned helplessness". This is where students feel failure is inevitable, as they feel powerless and that they have no control over the situation. This can lead to them withdrawing early. In this mindset, disappointment quickly turns into resentment and then ultimately into disengagement. This may well be accompanied by having a high fear of failure and low self-esteem in the long run.

If students know multiple ways to solve a problem, then when one way doesn't work, they can move on to an alternative method. This gets to the essence of what it means to be resilient, i.e. not being demotivated after a setback as you know what you would do differently next time. It's not enough to want to get better and succeed, it's knowing the tools and strategies for how to do so that matters.

The big caveat when it comes to teaching students multiple strategies to solve a problem is not to rush students to this phase. Doing so all at once, especially at the beginning of their learning journey, can cause cognitive overload. The aim has to be to build knowledge and application of these strategies over time.

The Watson Matrix

Illuminated by @Inner_Drive | innerdrive.co.uk

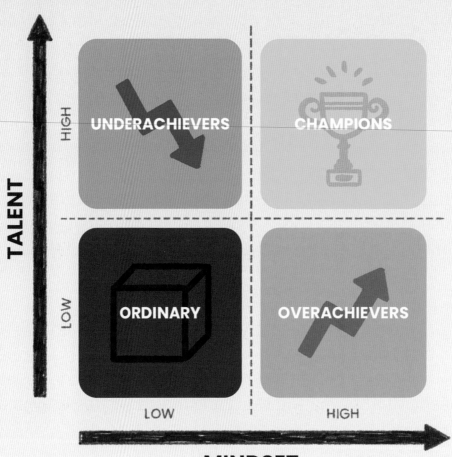

TALENT

HIGH · **UNDERACHIEVERS** · **CHAMPIONS**

LOW · **ORDINARY** · **OVERACHIEVERS**

LOW · HIGH

MINDSET

Underachievers
Talent potential is left unfulfilled due to self-sabotaging behaviours and making poor decisions.

Champions
Truly great achievements require both incredible talent and an elite mindset towards self-improvement.

Ordinary
With not much talent and a terrible attitude towards learning, it is very difficult to do well.

Overachievers
Hard work and learning from mistakes allow them to achieve more than some may have expected them to.

THE WATSON MATRIX

The "Watson Matrix" is the first graphic we ever designed at InnerDrive. It was born out of an attempt to explain to students how both talent and mindset interact for one's success.

In the Watson Matrix, talent refers to natural ability, intelligence, IQ and essentially what you are born with. It is largely genetic and based on one's DNA. Mindset, on the other hand, refers to one's attitude, work ethic, optimism, and ability to learn from setbacks and mistakes. It is essentially what you do with your talent.

We have seen some students fall prey to the "talent myth" in that they believe that is the only factor that will determine their success or failure ("I am so clever I don't need to work hard" vs "I am so dumb it doesn't matter what I do, I will still fail this exam").

Likewise, we also think it is disingenuous to only talk about the importance of mindset, as we know that genetic factors will always interact and play a part. This graphic helps remind students that it is not, and will never be, exclusively talent or mindset. However, the one that they have the most control over is their mindset, as small daily choices that we make add up to form our mindset.

We often emphasise to students that the aim may not necessarily be to end up in the top right box. Education, and indeed life, is about helping ensure we end up in either of the right-hand boxes. If they do this, it means we have helped them to maximise what they have got, and on occasions, to succeed beyond what they thought was possible.

Now of course this model is simplistic. We know that factors such as luck and chance play a huge role (so in truth there should be a third axis). It is not a complete or holistic diagram. But what it does do, which all good diagrams should, is it helps to start a conversation. It helps summarise an idea, or set of ideas, in a way that is quick and clear to understand.

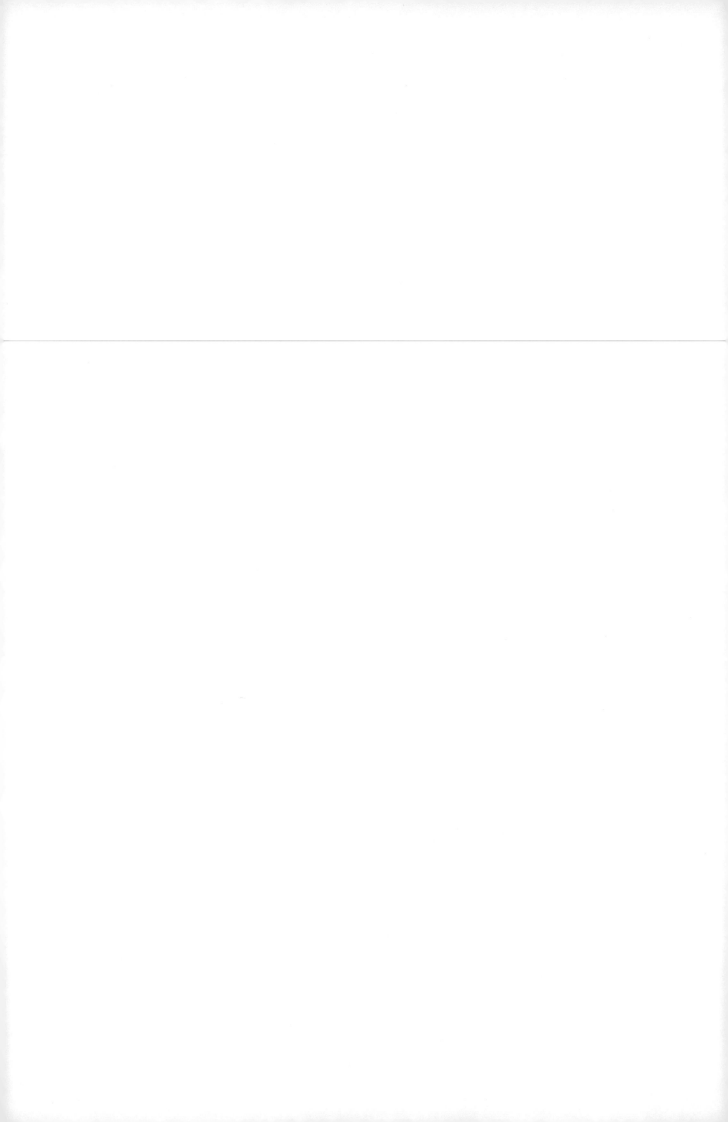

Preparing to Learn

The hidden factors that contribute to how much you learn.

DOI: 10.4324/9781003334361-10

The negative impact of phones on students

Inspired by Carl Hendrick | Illuminated by @Inner_Drive | innerdrive.co.uk

🇺🇸 USA
Bjornsen & Archer
2015

Using phones a lot in class had a negative impact on student test scores, regardless of past academic achievement.

🇬🇧 United Kingdom
Beland & Murphy
2016

Schools that banned mobile phones got an increase in GCSE results especially for underachieving students.

🇪🇸 Spain
Beneito & Vicente-Chivirella
2020

Banning phones in schools was associated with an increase in Maths and Science grades, as well as a reduction in bullying.

🇧🇷 Brazil
Felisoni & Godoi
2017

For every 100 minutes spent on a phone, a student's class ranking dropped significantly.

🇳🇴 Norway
Guldvik & Kvinnsland
2018

Banning mobile phones in schools led to a reduction in bullying among the students.

🇮🇳 India
Bhatt et al
2017

Higher levels of phone usage by college students were linked to reduced quality of sleep.

🇿🇦 South Africa
Porter et al
2015

55% of students who had used a mobile phone within the last 12 months had experienced cyber-bullying via their phone.

🇳🇬 Nigeria
Adeleke
2017

There was a correlation between increased time spent on phones and decreased academic achievement.

🇨🇳 China
Liu et al
2020

Phone use of 2+ hours on a weekday and 5+ hours on a weekend led to worse grades in Maths and English.

🇲🇾 Malaysia
Ng et al
2017

The more time students spent on their phone, even for learning activities, the lower their grade point average.

🇦🇺 Australia
Winskel et al
2019

There was a negative relationship between how much students used their phone and their grade.

THE NEGATIVE IMPACT OF PHONES ON STUDENTS

Let us be under no illusion, there is a mobile phone crisis in the world today. Research has found that being on your mobile phone too much negatively hinders your ability to concentrate, reduces the quality and quantity of sleep, whilst increasing stress and fear of missing out (FOMO). The data discussed in this graphic has been collected from a range of studies, research papers and surveys. It really does highlight the extent of this mobile phone addiction and problem.

When exploring any teaching and learning policy (and especially any that involves technology), the question of "how confident are we that this will lead to a learning gain?" must be asked. Although possible to have a net positive if managed very carefully, there is now a wealth of evidence that mobile phones in the classroom actually lead to a learning loss. This is before we even get to issues such as pastoral, well-being and safeguarding concerns, as well as the practical and logistical issues.

Given that so many students are on their mobile phone for such long periods of time and feel stressed when apart from it, it is good to reflect on what they are doing whilst on it. The truth is these devices shouldn't be called mobile phones, as arguably this is one of the features they use the least. We cannot get away from the worrying research finding that a large chunk of time on these devices is spent on social media, gaming and accessing pornography. When we view it in those terms, as opposed to it being a mobile telephone, the time spent on it and attachment to it should be viewed in a more worrying light.

It is hard to look at this graphic and come to the conclusion that students need to be on their phone more. If anything, schools have the potential to offer a safe haven and respite from the "always being on" phenomenon experienced by our students. Given that so many check their phones straight away in the morning and sleep next to it at night, not having mobile phones in the classroom might be a prudent and worthwhile policy to explore.

Designing brilliant PowerPoint slides

Illuminated by @Inner_Drive | innerdrive.co.uk

1. Focus their attention on what matters

Finally, you can read this

READ THIS FIRST

Then read this.

Then read this once you have read the bigger, bolder, more contrasted text.

2. Avoid redundant information

REMOVE UNNECESSARY WORDS ~~THAT YOU DON'T NEED~~ IN SENTENCES.

3. If using images, make them big enough to be seen

HERMANN EBBINGHAUS

Ebbinghaus was born 24 January 1850 in Barmen.

He was a German psychologist, known for his work on memory and in particular for his discovery of the forgetting curve.

He died 26 February 1909.

HERMANN EBBINGHAUS

- Born 24/01/1850
- German psychologist working on memory.
- Discovered the forgetting curve.
- Died 26/02/1909

DESIGNING BRILLIANT POWERPOINT SLIDES

PowerPoint was not designed with teaching and learning in mind. Originally created in 1984 and first released by Microsoft in the early 1990s, it was intended to be used in short business meetings as a presentational tool. It now dominates the classroom as well.

Despite its popularity, it is frightening to think how little training is dedicated to how to use it. As a result, it is often used in ways that were never intended and have since been found to be in contrast to how we know people remember information. As Professor Richard Mayer, best known for his research on cognitive load theory, once stated, "in light of the science, it is up to us to make a fundamental shift in our thinking – we can no longer expect people to struggle to try to adapt to our PowerPoint habits to align with the way people learn".

Given our limited focus and finite working memory capacity, it is important to draw students' attention to the most important piece of information on the slide. This is known as the "Signalling Principle" and can be done with clear, large and bold headings, as well as with the use of subtitles. Likewise, removing excessive words is likely to help reduce the visual load placed on students. PowerPoint slides shouldn't be thought of as a script, but instead as a prompt, with the detail being narrated by the teacher. If we do need to give large amounts of information, physical handouts are likely to be better.

The Multimedia Principle states that people learn better with a combination of pictures and words. However, if you are using images, it is important to make them prominent enough on the slide. If not, they are just clutter. These images need to be relevant and related to the key content. If they are not, then they can be distracting (which is a nod to the Coherence Effect discussed earlier in this book).

The cost of multi-tasking

Illuminated by @Inner_Drive | innerdrive.co.uk

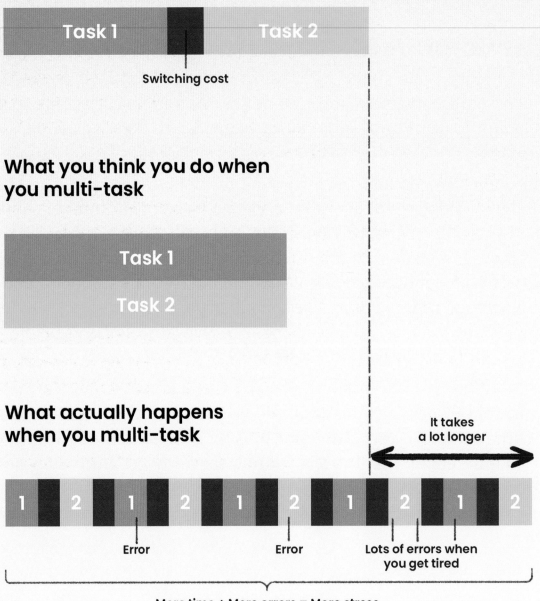

What you should do

Task 1 | Switching cost | Task 2

Switching cost

What you think you do when you multi-task

Task 1

Task 2

What actually happens when you multi-task

1 2 1 2 1 2 1 2 1 2 1 2

It takes a lot longer

Error

Error

Lots of errors when you get tired

More time + More errors = More stress

THE COST OF MULTI-TASKING

Multi-tasking is a myth. That is to say, conscious multi-tasking is a myth. Any time that you are required to do two separate tasks that require your focus, it takes time, effort and energy switching between the two. This has three consequences: it increases stress, reduces performance and leads to more errors.

When most students think they are multi-tasking, what they are actually doing is switching between tasks very quickly. This is stressful, as it places an extra cognitive load due to their attention being split. This process can be fatiguing, as the mental resources required are overburdened by the constant juggling act this task-switching requires.

It is important to emphasise that our students are living in an age of distraction. It is sadly too common for many of them to do their homework with a range of interruptions right next to them. This may include their phone, numerous tabs open, listening to music or watching YouTube/TV/Netflix in the background.

In a curious twist of fate, research suggests that students who multi-task the most are actually the worst at it. This means that they are often more distracted and struggle to filter out irrelevant distractors. Furthermore, research has found that around 70% of students feel that they have an above-average ability to multi-task. Taken together this suggests that it may be a bigger problem than perhaps many of them realise.

Students may seek comfort in these intrusions on their focus. But the inevitable truth is that if accuracy matters, it is better to do one thing, finish it, and then do another, as opposed to pretending (a) that they can multi-task and (b) that it is better for them and their learning.

How to use the Cornell Note Taking Method

Illuminated by @Inner_Drive | innerdrive.co.uk

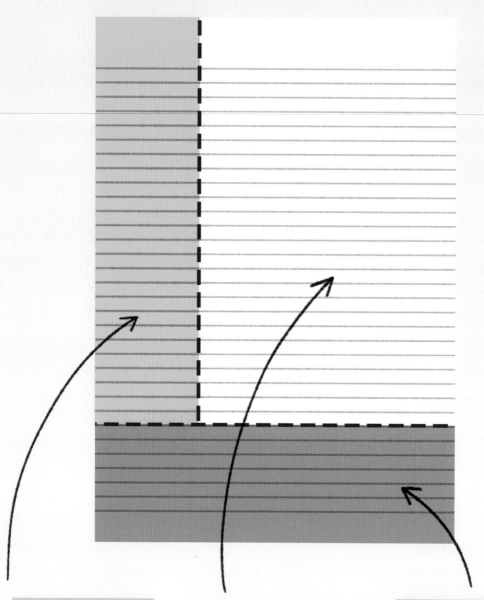

1. **Cue column**

- Key words
- Ask questions
- Prompts for studying

2. **Note column**

- Make notes
- Summarise concepts

3. **Summary**

- Review what you have learnt

Reference: Pauk, 1962

HOW TO USE THE CORNELL NOTE TAKING METHOD

The Cornell Note Taking Method was first devised by Walter Pauk, who in the 1950s worked at Cornell University. Even though this method is over 70 years old, recent research has found that it can still provide an effective method for helping students.

To use the Cornell Note Taking Method, students need to divide their page into three sections. There are two vertical columns, one thin and one wide, with the former taking up about 30% of the width and the latter taking up the remaining 70%. These provide space for key words/questions and then for the main body of notes.

The bottom horizontal section is where students summarise and review what they have learnt. This is an important feature of this method, as it allows students to tie in the key points covered, helping them make connections and links with prior learning. If done after the lesson or at the end of the day, it also provides another opportunity to review their notes before they forget what they have learnt, tapping in to the Spacing Effect.

There is some debate about the extent to which this method of note taking has a direct effect on students' academic achievements. What it certainly does do is provide a clear structure and prompt on how to take notes. Evidence suggests that taking notes of what the teacher says verbatim leads to a shallower processing of the information. Having to summarise their learning in their own words encourages students to think harder about the content and so internalise it more effectively.

The other advantage of the Cornell Note Taking Method is that it provides a base for further retrieval practice. As well as helping students to replicate the notes from memory at a later date, writing a list of key questions helps students generate study quizzes for them to answer, thus improving their retrieval practice.

The psychology behind seating plans

Illuminated by @Inner_Drive | innerdrive.co.uk

A great seating plan helps students[1]...

 ...stay more on track and focused on the task at hand.

 ... display more positive academic behaviours.

 ...form better peer relationships.

Choose your seating plan based on:

The nature of the task
Individual assignment or group work?

The desired behaviour
Focus or discussion?

Rows

Better if you want order and independent work

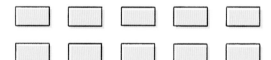

- Foster a quieter environment
- Less distraction, more focus
- More on-task behaviour and less disruptive behaviour for students with SEN[2]

Groups

Better if you want to reap the benefits of group work

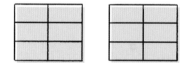

- Students are more likely to brainstorm
- Better work on group assignments
- Encourage students to ask more questions, which helps them learn a topic faster

---

Don't let students choose where to sit.

This creates much more disruption than when the teacher chooses, as students tend to sit near friends[3].

Do sit weaker students near hard workers.

Bandwagon Effect: If someone near you is working hard, even on a different task, you tend to work harder too.

Köhler Effect: Surprisingly, strong students tend to pull weaker ones up, rather than the latter dragging the former down.

Do sit distracted students behind more attentive ones.

Having an attentive student in their field of vision causes students to take more notes and have a better memory of the material that is being taught[4].

References: [1]Wannarka & Ruhl, 2008   [2]Wheldall & Lam, 1987   [3]Bicard et al, 2012   [4]Forrin et al, 2021

THE PSYCHOLOGY BEHIND SEATING PLANS

Did you know that research has found that when students choose their own seats, they are twice as disruptive compared with when the teachers decide the seating arrangements? Other research indicates that a good seating plan can help students stay more focused on the task at hand, be more likely to ask for help when they need it and develop better peer-to-peer relations.

A significant part of the decision comes down to rows vs groups. Evidence suggests that rows lead to quieter environments and fewer distractions. Likewise, another study found that rows may be beneficial for students with special educational needs, as it increases concentration and reduces disruptions. That being said, group tables have been associated with an increase in brainstorming and work for group assignments. They also promote an increase in asking questions.

Within either rows or groups, there is a fascinating psychology at play to factor in when deciding who sits next to who. A range of studies have found that if students are strategically placed in close proximity to someone who is paying attention or working hard, they are more likely to do so themselves. This is akin to the Bandwagon Effect, which describes how we tend to adopt the behaviours of the group.

Likewise, the Köhler Effect describes how when two or more people complete a joint task, the weaker individual of the two tends to perform better compared with if they had done it alone. This means that the weaker of the pair is elevated, as opposed to the stronger being dragged down.

Seating plans can clearly play a big role in affecting classroom culture, behaviour and habits. It will likely come down to a judgement call, as it is not an exact science. Hopefully, though, research from psychology can help inform some of those decisions.

What All Teachers (But Especially Senior Leaders) Need to Know

Key factors to consider when deciding on interventions.

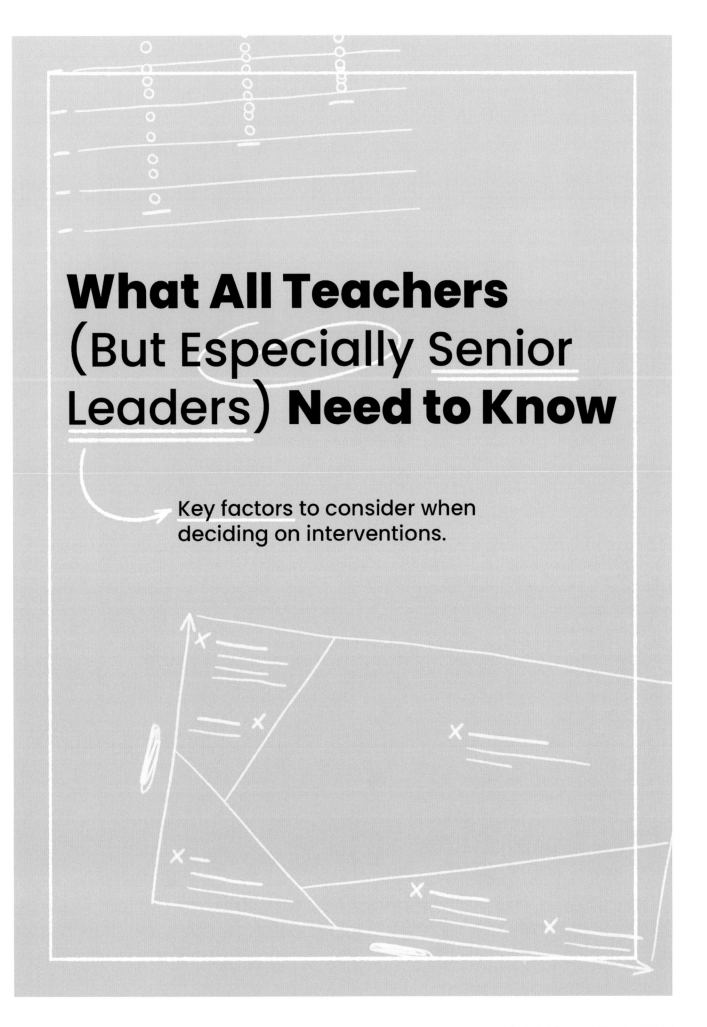

DOI: 10.4324/9781003334361-11

How to spend your time

Illuminated by @Inner_Drive | innerdrive.co.uk

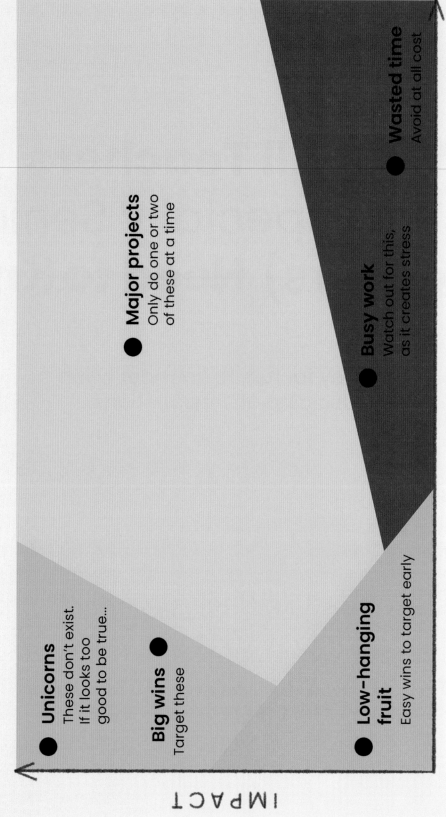

Unicorns
These don't exist.
If it looks too
good to be true...

Big wins
Target these

Low-hanging fruit
Easy wins to target early

Major projects
Only do one or two
of these at a time

Busy work
Watch out for this,
as it creates stress

Wasted time
Avoid at all cost

IMPACT

EFFORT

HOW TO SPEND YOUR TIME

Time is the most precious resource in education. It constantly feels that there is never enough of it. With such a limited resource, it has to be spent wisely. Every decision, intervention and strategy has an opportunity cost. This graphic, which echoes the famous Eisenhower Matrix, provides a framework for how to divide our time.

Strategies that are high on effort and low on impact are at best busy work, and at worst, wasted time. These can be stressful and should be avoided at all costs. They give the illusion of progress but in reality result in people burning out in frustration at little progress being made.

On the other end of the spectrum, strategies that require almost no effort and have a high impact probably don't exist (hence why we have labelled them "Unicorns"). "Low-hanging fruit" and "Big wins" are ones that have a good impact-to-effort ratio. The former can help start building positive momentum, with the latter driving significant change. These are both very good places to start.

"Major projects" are ones that require a significant amount of effort and yield a notable impact. There are only a limited amount of these you can do at a given time, as they require a clear vision, strategy, and above all, time to plan. Doing too many at once probably lowers the quality of each, which results in a reduction of impact.

Sometimes it can be hard to deduce in advance where a project sits on this graphic. It involves a lot of guesswork and a little bit of luck. Reflecting on previous similar tasks, as well as asking a range of trusted and diverse sources, probably offers the best route to doing so accurately.

The Relative Age Effect

Illuminated by @Inner _Drive | innerdrive.co.uk

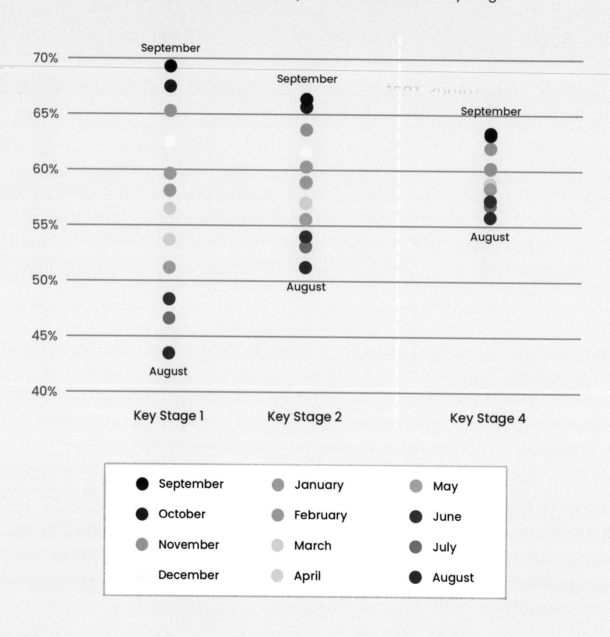

% achieving expected standard by month of birth and key stage

Reference: FFT Education Datalab, 2017

THE RELATIVE AGE EFFECT

The Relative Age Effect describes how students who are born early in the academic year perform to a higher level than those who are born later. It has been studied extensively in a wide range of fields, but specifically in sport and education.

A version of this graphic was originally published by the Education Datalab, which showed what percentage of students were achieving the expected standard in Key Stage 1, Key Stage 2 and Key Stage 4 by the month they were born in. There are two things that instantly jump off the page when viewing this graphic.

The first is just how large the gap is between September-born students and August-born students in Key Stage 1. A difference of over 25 percentage points based on age is a huge variation. It is interesting to consider at what age students have labels attached to them (i.e. smart, intelligent, gifted and talented). Could it be, for the most part, especially at an early age, we are often simply confusing intelligence with age?

Why might findings like this matter so much? If younger students are consistently behind their older peers in terms of academic achievement, and the reason for this is not well understood, then it may lead to those younger students developing a negative self-concept, which in turn can lead to a self-fulfilling prophecy around not being smart enough to do well in education.

The second thing that stands out is that, thankfully, the gap between the eldest and the youngest in the year gets smaller. This is presumably because the percentage difference in age decreases, so factors like their intelligence and hard work carry more weight. Evidence from other studies has found that a few years later, the gap is even smaller in terms of university admissions.

What All Teachers (But Especially Primary Teachers) Need to Know

Teaching & learning strategies that make a big difference early on in a student's academic career.

DOI: 10.4324/9781003334361-12

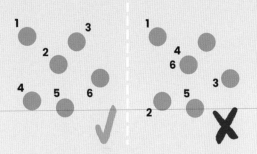

The one-to-one principle

Each item in a group is counted only once.

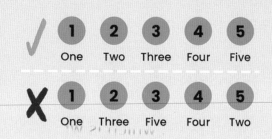

The stable order principle

When counting, the names of numbers remain in the same order.

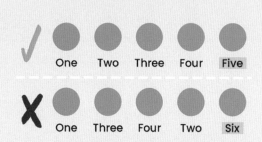

The cardinal principle

The final number said when counting represents the total number in a group.

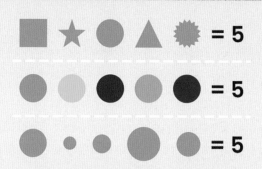

The abstraction principle

We count a collection of items the same way, regardless of their characteristics.

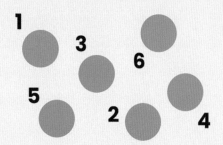

The order irrelevance principle

The counting order doesn't matter as long as we follow the other principles.

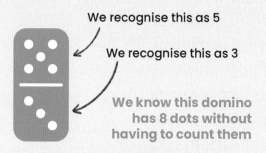

We recognise this as 5

We recognise this as 3

We know this domino has 8 dots without having to count them

Subitising

The ability to determine numerosity without having to consciously count.

THE SCIENCE OF COUNTING

Numbers can be quite an abstract concept, and until children learn the principles that underpin how to count correctly, numbers can be challenging for them to understand. These principles cover how to count (i.e. the One-to-One, Stable Order and Cardinal principles) and what to count (i.e. the Abstraction and Order Irrelevance principles).

The One-to-One Principle is fundamental because young students have the tendency to either "skim", which is when they miss an object due to counting too quickly, or "flurry", which is when they count the same item several times. The Stable Order Principle helps mitigate the trickiness of the English language, as the names of numbers don't always have a pattern. For example, eleven, twelve, thirteen and fifteen don't follow the same "rule" as fourteen, sixteen, seventeen, eighteen and nineteen.

Research suggests that the Cardinal Principle is important, as it can provide a platform for other counting skills (i.e. the "later-greater principle"). Evidence suggests that a number of factors are associated with mastering the Cardinal Principle. These include IQ, number of count words known, as well as preliteracy skills. Likewise, the Abstraction Principle helps develop a deeper understanding of counting as evidence suggests that students find it easier to count tangible concepts compared with abstract ones.

The Order Irrelevance Principle teaches students that it does not matter if you count objects from left to right, right to left, top to bottom, or bottom to top (or any other variation really), it will not change the total number of items. That being said, some evidence suggests that applying this principle early when students start learning to count may produce a cognitive overload and tax their working memory, and as such, it may be more useful only when they have learnt to count automatically.

Subitising is technically not a counting principle. However, it does rely on ability with the other principles, and as such, can be a useful indicator of the student's proficiency in counting.

Metacognitive questions: before, during and after

Adapted from Jade Powers | Illuminated by @Inner_Drive | innerdrive.co.uk

1. Before – Knowledge
- Do I understand what this task is asking me to do?
- Have I previously completed a similar task?

YES
- What mistakes do I usually make when completing tasks like this?
- What can I learn from my last attempt?
- What is the best approach to use with this task?

NO
- What skills and knowledge can I use to help me approach this task?
- Which resources can I use to help me be successful?

2. During – Regulation
- Am I finding anything difficult right now?

YES
- Why am I finding it difficult?
- Can I use any previous examples for support?

NO
- What am I doing well?
- How do I know I'm doing well?
- Does my work look successful?

3. After – Reflection
- Did I feel motivated during that task?
- Am I happy with the work I have completed?

YES
- What motivated me?
- How can I learn from this experience for next time?

NO
- Which emotions did I feel during this task?
- What would I do differently next time?

Metacognitive questions can help students:
- Take more ownership
- Increase their motivation
- Enhance self-regulation
- Develop self-awareness
- Become better independent learners

METACOGNITIVE QUESTIONS: BEFORE, DURING AND AFTER

Ever since the Education Endowment Foundation Toolkit highlighted metacognition as one of the most cost-effective ways to help students improve their learning, more and more schools have started to try to develop their students' metacognitive skills.

Metacognition is often referred to as "thinking about thinking". We think this can be expanded upon to cover a student's ability to be aware of what they know, what they are thinking about, and choose a helpful thought process. It is often divided into three sections: before, during and after a task. This "before, during and after" approach is very similar to the "plan-do-review" mantra which is heavily used in elite sport, business and in the army.

Encouraging students to ask themselves rich metacognitive questions is a strategy that can be applied at each of these three stages. This is because at each stage certain questions can help activate previous learning and help students to reflect on which strategies and processes have been most helpful and effective. As a result, they are more likely to do the task more effectively.

As with most of the other strategies and interventions listed in this book, the skill is in the application of it. It is more a case of the "how and when" than the "what". If students know how these questions will help and when they should ask them, it transforms the potential and effectiveness of these metacognitive questions.

Asking questions before a task can help ready students to learn, by helping them make comparisons with previous similar events. Asking self-questions during a task can help keep students on course, ensuring they are monitoring their performance. Finally, evaluative questions afterwards can help prompt self-reflection. Taken together, all three stages can help students take more ownership of their learning.

Rethinking Maslow's Hierarchy of Needs

Illuminated by @Inner_Drive | innerdrive.co.uk

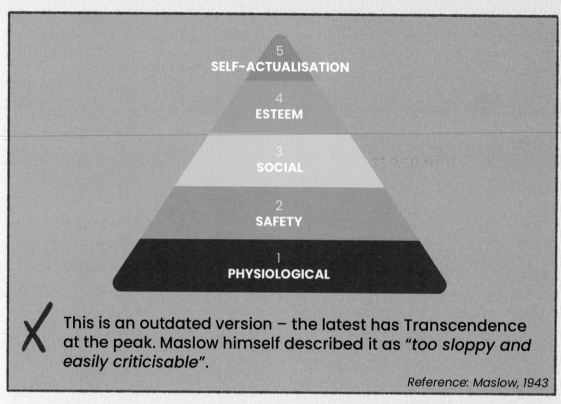

This is an outdated version – the latest has Transcendence at the peak. Maslow himself described it as *"too sloppy and easily criticisable"*.

Reference: Maslow, 1943

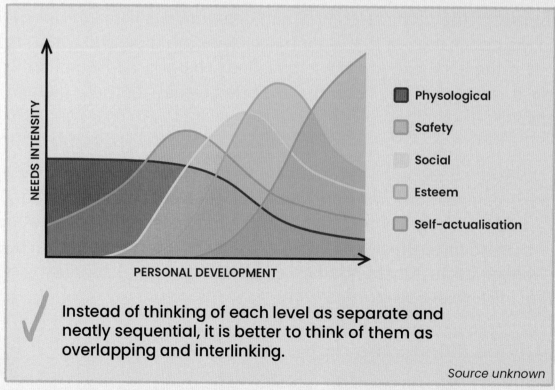

Instead of thinking of each level as separate and neatly sequential, it is better to think of them as overlapping and interlinking.

Source unknown

RETHINKING MASLOW'S HIERARCHY OF NEEDS

Maslow's Hierarchy of Needs has by and large stood the test of time. It was first released during World War Two and sought to explore the direction of travel one goes through in terms of motivation in order to fulfil one's motivation. Essentially, one's physiological and primary needs must be met before one can meet the "higher order" psychological needs.

Maslow's hierarchy of needs is better than most educational pyramids and certainly passes the first-glance-eye-test, in so much as it follows the expected rules of a pyramid; one has to "complete" the previous level in order to progress to the next one.

However, it is worth noting that all is not rosy in the Maslow garden. A number of other researchers have commented that instead of thinking of each level as separate and perfectly sequential, it is probably more accurate to think of them as overlapping and at times interlinking, meaning that it may be more complex than usually presented.

Another area of caution in relation to Maslow's hierarchy of needs to be aware of is that there exists a more detailed update that is less well known than the famous original version. Published just before Maslow's death (which partly explains why it registers less in the public's consciousness), it includes additional layers, one of which has "Transcendence" at the peak instead of "Self-Actualisation". It has been reported that Maslow felt his original model was "too sloppy and easily criticisable" and that he "meant to write and publish a self-actualisation critique, but somehow never did". Transcendence includes helping others develop their potential, whereas Self-Actualisation tends to focus more on realising one's own individual potential.

Overall, this model certainly isn't perfect. It has its flaws and weaknesses, and like all pyramid models is too "neat" to be considered true. That being said, it is worth knowing about (and indeed using in this visual demonstration) as it does provide a strong platform to help initially understand a range of areas that include but are not limited to intrinsic motivation, psychological safety and attachment in students.

Thinking Biases

Quirks of the brain that can have a
big impact on how we think and learn.

DOI: 10.4324/9781003334361-13

Types of thinking biases

Inspired by designhacks.co | Illuminated by @Inner_Drive | innerdrive.co.uk

Learning Errors

We avoid using tools from external sources, are over-reliant on how we've previously worked, and forget what we look up on the internet.

Ability

We value natural talent, overestimate our own, and find it hard to recall being a novice.

Own Ideas

We seek information that confirms our initial opinions, make current decisions to justify our past ones, and place too much emphasis on our own creations.

Time

We place too much weight on our first & last impressions, and things often take more time than we think.

Change

We feel better if we are doing something, want to protect the status quo, and find new, conflicting evidence hard to process.

Others

We tend to follow the crowd, think everyone is paying attention to us more than they are, and change our behaviour when observed.

New information

We listen to people who are similar to us, try to ignore bad news, and think we are immune to thinking biases.

Results

We judge our decisions based on the outcome, over-remember the success stories, and are more sensitive to negative things.

Google Effect
Not Invented Here Effect
Talent Bias
Dunning-Kruger Effect
Curse of Expertise
Halo Effect
Recency Effect
Planning Fallacy
Spotlight Effect
Bandwagon Effect
Hawthorne Effect
Outcome Bias
Survivorship Bias
Negativity Bias
In vs Out Group
Ostrich Effect
Blind Spot Bias
Action Bias
Conservatism Bias
Status Bias
Confirmation Bias
Sunk-Cost Fallacy
Ikea Effect
Law of the Instrument

TYPES OF THINKING BIASES

Most teaching and learning books do not contain information about thinking biases, as they haven't been studied extensively in education yet. And yet, they are often the silent assassins that can severely restrict learning, as our own (and our students') thought processes are not always the clearest or the most rational.

To date, researchers have found over 175 different types of thinking biases that we suffer from. Our graphic includes arguably the 24 most common ones in education. Each on their own can hinder student learning, but combined together they can be devastating.

These thinking biases can be divided into views about our ability, perception of time, impact of others, what the result was, why we reject new information, why change is difficult, why we love our own ideas, and faulty beliefs about learning. But the common thread they have is they all anchor in one partial piece of information over all others. This can cloud our judgement as we have excessively anchored in either irrelevant or partial parts of the information available.

The curious (and indeed frustrating) thing about these thinking biases is we all have them and yet they are much easier to spot in other people than in ourselves. This makes overcoming them ourselves difficult. And yet we must if we are to best help our students. It is difficult to innovate, be research-informed and evidence-based if these thinking biases stop us from thinking rationally and logically, as they can lead to ill-thought-out interventions and make for suboptimal evaluations of them.

There is no easy or quick way to overcome these thinking biases, as most of the time we don't even realise they are happening. But it is possible to help mitigate their effects. First, we have to acknowledge we all have these biases, as intelligence/wealth/race/gender does not make any of us immune to them. Secondly, by interacting with a diverse range of people (both in terms of experience and background) we can escape our own echo chambers, which tend to be fertile breeding grounds for thinking biases.

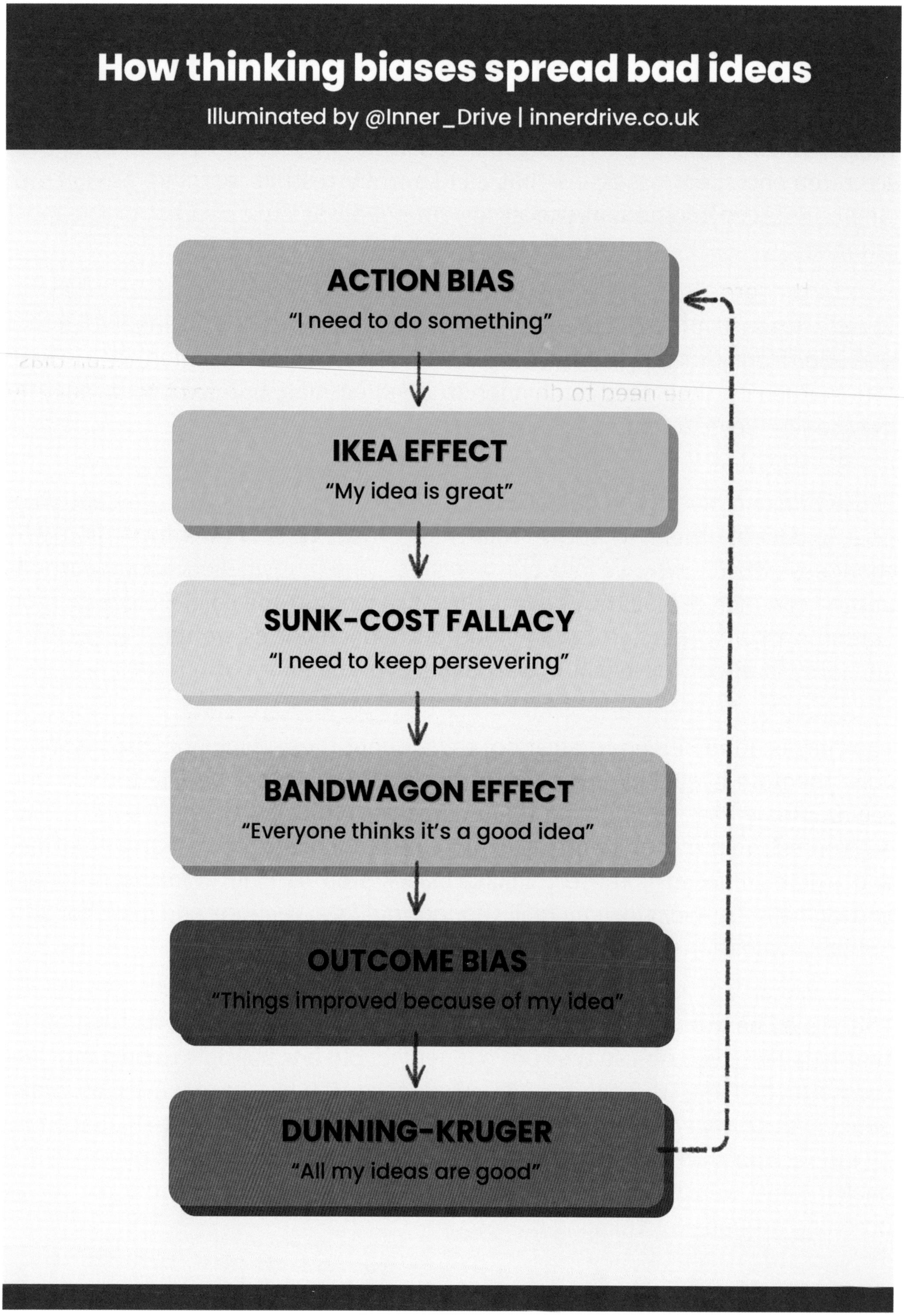
How thinking biases spread bad ideas
Illuminated by @Inner_Drive | innerdrive.co.uk
ACTION BIAS
"I need to do something"
IKEA EFFECT
"My idea is great"
SUNK-COST FALLACY
"I need to keep persevering"
BANDWAGON EFFECT
"Everyone thinks it's a good idea"
OUTCOME BIAS
"Things improved because of my idea"
DUNNING-KRUGER
"All my ideas are good"

HOW THINKING BIASES SPREAD BAD IDEAS

Teaching & Learning has certainly seen its fair share of well-intended but ultimately ill-conceived interventions aimed at improving students' educational achievements. Some of these neuromyths stubbornly persist and refuse to die (hence why they are referred to by some as "zombie myths").

Due to the large range of thinking biases, we can map out a potential path as to how these bad ideas grow and spread. It often starts with the noble idea of wanting to do something to help improve the situation. Due to an "Action Bias", this morphs into the need to do anything. It is akin to being seen to be busy. As people tend to over-value their own creations (the IKEA Effect), as well as seeking out evidence that supports their opinion, momentum quickly gathers.

The Sunk-Cost Fallacy describes how we sometimes persist with a course of action even if it is sub-optimal. As we persevere, over time more people may say it looks like a good idea, which enables the Bandwagon Effect, where an outsider assumes it must be a good idea because many others say it is.

Working out if a specific intervention or strategy has directly led to the desired outcome is notoriously tricky. Often, we can confuse correlation with causation. It is therefore easy to assume a positive outcome was due to our intervention (i.e. Outcome Bias). Under these conditions, it is easy to see how we can get an over-inflated view of our abilities (the Dunning-Kruger Effect). This can lead to a vicious cycle where we want to carry out more interventions as we have "the golden touch", leading to the original Action Bias kicking in.

For too long, fads and gimmicks have dominated the education landscape. Neuromyths may be the spark, but it is the thinking biases that we are all susceptible to that help them spread like wildfire.

In case you got this far

What to do next now that
you've finished reading
Teaching & Learning Illuminated.

Should you recommend this book to a colleague?

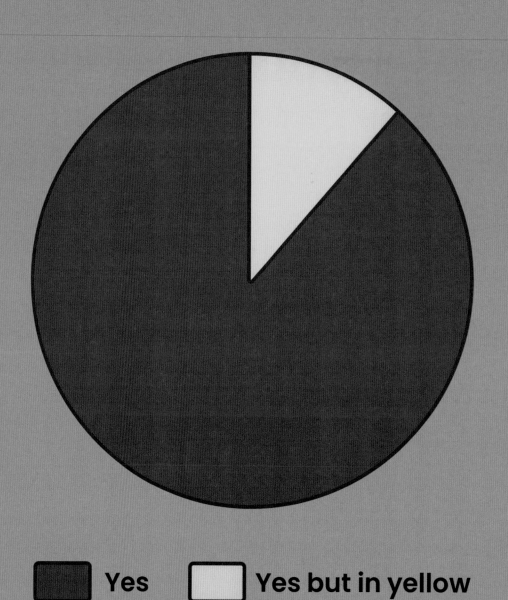

Yes   Yes but in yellow

Where to find out more

Scan this QR code
to access all of InnerDrive's
free teaching & learning resources

STUDIES, BOOKS AND ARTICLES THAT INSPIRED AND INFLUENCED US

Abel, M., & Bäuml, K. H. T. (2020). Would you like to learn more? Retrieval practice plus feedback can increase motivation to keep on studying. *Cognition*, 201, 104316.

Aben, B., Stapert, S., & Blokland, A. (2012). About the distinction between working memory and short-term memory. *Frontiers in Psychology*, 3, 301.

Adeleke, A. G. (2017). Influence of time-on-phone on undergraduates' academic achievement in Nigerian universities. *American Journal of Educational Research*, 5(5), 564-567.

Agarwal, P. K., D'Antonio, L., Roediger III, H. L., McDermott, K. B., & McDaniel, M. A. (2014). Classroom-based programs of retrieval practice reduce middle school and high school students' test anxiety. *Journal of Applied Research in Memory and Cognition*, 3(3), 131-139.

Agasisti, T. et al. (2018). Academic resilience: What schools and countries do to help disadvantaged students succeed in PISA. *OECD Education Working Papers*, No. 167, OECD.

Allen, J., Gregory, A., Mikami, A., Lun, J., Hamre, B., & Pianta, R. (2013). Observations of effective teacher-student interactions in secondary school classrooms: Predicting student achievement with the classroom assessment scoring system - secondary. *School Psychology Review*, 42(1), 76-98.

Ariely, D., & Wertenbroch, K. (2002). Procrastination, deadlines, and performance: Self-control by pre-commitment. *Psychological Science*, 13(3), 219-224.

Asch, S. E. (1951). Effects of group pressure upon the modification and distortion of judgments. In H. Guetzkow (Ed.), *Groups, Leadership and Men: Research in Human Relations* (pp. 177-190). Oxford: Carnegie Press.

Atir, S., Rosenzweig, E., & Dunning, D. (2015). When knowledge knows no bounds: Self-perceived expertise predicts claims of impossible knowledge. *Psychological Science*, 26(8), 1295-1303.

Atkinson, C., & Mayer, R. E. (2004). Five ways to reduce PowerPoint overload. *Creative Commons*, 1(1), 1-15.

Ayres, P. (2013). Can the isolated-elements strategy be improved by targeting points of high cognitive load for additional practice? *Learning and Instruction*, 23, 115-124.

Beland, L. P., & Murphy, R. (2016). Ill communication: Technology, distraction & student performance. *Labour Economics*, 41, 61-76.

Benassi, V. A., Overson, C. E., & Hakala, C. M. (2014). *Applying Science of Learning in Education: Infusing Psychological Science into the Curriculum*. Society for the Teaching of Psychology.

Beneito, P., & Vicente-Chirivella, O. (2020). Banning mobile phones at schools: Effects on bullying and academic performance. *Discussion Papers in Economic Behaviour*.

Beranuy, M., Oberst, U., Carbonell, X., & Chamarro, A. (2009). Problematic Internet and mobile phone use and clinical symptoms in college students: The role of emotional intelligence. *Computers in Human Behavior*, 25(5), 1182-1187.

Berman, M. G., Jonides, J., & Kaplan, S. (2008). The cognitive benefits of interacting with nature. *Psychological Science*, 19(12), 1207-1212.

Bhatt, N., Muninarayanappa, N. V., & Nageshwar, V. (2017). A study to assess the mobile phone dependence level and sleep quality among students of selected colleges of Moradabad. *Indian Journal of Public Health Research & Development*, 8(1), 41.

Bicard, D. F., Ervin, A., Bicard, S. C., & Baylot-Casey, L. (2012). Differential effects of seating arrangements on disruptive behavior of fifth grade students during independent seatwork. *Journal of Applied Behavior Analysis*, 45(2), 407-411.

Bjornsen, C. A., & Archer, K. J. (2015). Relations between college students' cell phone use during class and grades. *Scholarship of Teaching and Learning in Psychology*, 1(4), 326-336.

Black, N., & de New, S. C. (2020). Short, heavy and underrated? Teacher assessment biases by children's body size. *Oxford Bulletin of Economics and Statistics*, 82(5), 961-987.

Bloom, B. (1956). *Taxonomy of Educational Objectives. Book I: Cognitive Domain*. New York: David McKay.

Blunt, A. K., & Pychyl, T. A. (2000). Task aversiveness and procrastination: A multi-dimensional approach to task aversiveness across stages of personal projects. *Personality and Individual Differences*, 28(1), 153-167.

Booth, J. L., McGinn, K. M., Young, L. K., & Barbieri, C. (2015). Simple practice doesn't always make perfect: Evidence from the Worked Example Effect. *Policy Insights from the Behavioral and Brain Sciences*, 2(1), 24-32.

Borman, G. D., Rozek, C. S., Pyne, J., & Hanselman, P. (2019). Reappraising academic and social adversity improves middle school students' academic achievement, behavior, and well-being. *Proceedings of the National Academy of Sciences*, 116(33), 16286-16291.

Boser, U. (2019). *What do teachers know about the science of learning? A survey of educators on how students learn*. The Learning Agency.

Brummelman, E., Thomaes, S., Nelemans, S., Orobio, B., Overbeek, G., & Bushman, B. (2015) Origins of narcissism in children. *PNAS*, 112(12), 3659-3662.

Buehler, R., Griffin, D., & Ross, M. (1994). Exploring the "Planning Fallacy": Why people underestimate their task completion times. *Journal of Personality and Social Psychology*, 67(3), 366-381.

Burgess, S., & Greaves, E. (2013). Test scores, subjective assessment, and stereotyping of ethnic minorities. *Journal of Labor Economics*, 31(3), 535-576.

Burnett, P. C. (1999). Children's self-talk and academic self-concepts: The impact of teachers' statements. *Educational Psychology in Practice*, 15(3), 195-200.

Butler, A. C. (2018). Multiple-choice testing in education: Are the best practices for assessment also good for learning? *Journal of Applied Research in Memory and Cognition*, 7(3), 323-331.

Butler, A. C., & Roediger, H. L. (2008). Feedback enhances the positive effects and reduces the negative effects of multiple-choice testing. *Memory & Cognition*, 36(3), 604-616.

Campbell, T. (2015). Stereotyped at seven? Biases in teachers' judgements of pupils' ability and attainment. *Journal of Social Policy*, 44(3), 517-547.

Carpenter, S., & Toftness, A. (2017). The effect of prequestions on learning from video presentations. *Journal of Applied Research in Memory and Cognition*, 6(1), 104-109.

Carpenter, S. K., Wiseheart, M., Rohrer, D., Kang, S. H., & Pashler, H. (2012). Using spacing to enhance diverse forms of learning: Review of recent research and implications for instruction. *Educational Psychology Review*, 24(3), 369-378.

Castro, M., Expósito-Casas, E., López-Martín, E., Lizasoain, L., Navarro-Asencio, E., & Gaviria, J. L. (2015). Parental involvement on student academic achievement: A meta-analysis. *Educational Research Review*, 14, 33-46.

Castro-Alonso, J. C., & Sweller, J. (2020). The modality effect of cognitive load theory. *Advances in Human Factors in Training, Education, and Learning Sciences*, 963, 75-84.

Centre for Education Statistics and Evaluation (CESE). (2018). Cognitive load theory in practice: Examples for the classroom.

Cepeda, N. J., Vul, E., Rohrer, D., Wixted, J. T., & Pashler, H. (2008). Spacing effects in learning: A temporal ridgeline of optimal retention. *Psychological Science*, 19(11), 1095-1102.

Chandler, P., & Sweller, J. (1992). The Split-Attention Effect as a factor in the design of instruction. *British Journal of Educational Psychology*, 62(2), 233-246.

Chen, O., Paas, F., & Sweller, J. (2021). Spacing and interleaving effects require distinct theoretical bases: A systematic review testing the cognitive load and discriminative-contrast hypotheses. *Educational Psychology Review*, 33(4), 1499-1522.

Chen, P., Chavez, O., Ong, D., & Gunderson, B. (2017). Strategic resource use for learning: A self-administered intervention that guides self-reflection on effective resource use enhances academic performance. *Psychological Science*, 28(6), 774-785.

Chew, S. L. (2021). An advance organizer for student learning: Choke points and pitfalls in studying. *Canadian Psychology*, 62(4), 420-427.

Chewprecha, T. (1980). Comparison of training methods in modifying questioning and wait time behaviors of Thai high school chemistry teachers. *Journal of Research in Science Teaching*, 17(3), 191-200.

Chong, T. S. (2005). Recent advances in cognitive load theory research: Implications for instructional designers. *Malaysian Online Journal of Instructional Technology (MOJIT)*, 2(3), 106-117.

Cierniak, G., Scheiter, K., & Gerjets, P. (2009). Explaining the split-attention effect: Is the reduction of extraneous cognitive load accompanied by an increase in germane cognitive load? *Computers in Human Behavior*, 25(2), 315-324.

Coe, R., Rauch, C. J., Kime, S., & Singleton, D. (2019). *Great Teaching Toolkit: Evidence Review*. Evidence Based Education.

Conroy, D. E., Poczwardowski, A., & Henschen, K. P. (2001). Evaluative criteria and emotional responses associated with failure and success among elite athletes and performing artists. *Journal of Applied Sport Psychology*, 13, 300-322.

Cooper, H., Nye, B., Charlton, K., Lindsay, J., & Greathouse, S. (1996). The effects of summer vacation on achievement test scores: A narrative and meta-analytic review. *Review of Educational Research*, 66(3), 227-268.

Cowan, N. (2009). What are the differences between long-term, short-term, and working memory? *Progress in Brain Research*, 169, 323-338.

Crum, A. J., Salovey, P., & Achor, S. (2013). Rethinking stress: The role of mindsets in determining the stress response. *Journal of Personality and Social Psychology*, 104(4), 716.

Dale, E. (1969). *Audio-Visual Methods in Teaching*. New York: Holt, Rinehart & Winston.

Dawson, C., & de Meza, D. (2018). Wishful thinking, prudent behavior: The evolutionary origin of optimism, loss aversion and disappointment aversion. SSRN Working Paper.

Deans for Impact. (2015). *The Science of Learning*. Deans for Impact.

De Berker, A. O., Rutledge, R. B., Mathys, C., Marshall, L., Cross, G. F., Dolan, R. J., & Bestmann, S. (2016). Computations of uncertainty mediate acute stress responses in humans. *Nature Communications*, 7(1), 1-11.

Desender, K., Beurms, S., & Van den Bussche, E. (2016). Is mental effort exertion contagious? *Psychonomic Bulletin & Review*, 23(2), 624-631.

Doty, C. M., Geraets, A. A., Wan, T., Saitta, E. K., & Chini, J. J. (2020). Student perspective of GTA strategies to reduce feelings of anxiousness with cold-calling. In *2019 Physics Education Research Conference Proceedings*.

Duckworth, A., Quinn, P., & Seligman, M. (2009). Positive predictors of teacher effectiveness. *Journal of Positive Psychology*, 4(6), 540-547.

Dunlosky, J., Rawson, K. A., Marsh, E. J., Nathan, M. J., & Willingham, D. T. (2013). Improving students' learning with effective learning techniques: Promising directions from cognitive and educational psychology. *Psychological Science in the Public Interest*, 14(1), 4-58.

Durkin, K., Star, J., & Rittle-Johnson, B. (2017). Using comparison of multiple strategies in the mathematics classroom: Lesson learned and next steps. *The International Journal of Mathematics Education*, 49(2).

Education Data Lab. (2017, March 3). Getting older quicker.

Epley, N., & Dunning, D. (2000). Feeling "holier than thou": Are self-serving assessments produced by errors in self or social prediction? *Journal of Personality and Social Psychology*, 79(6), 861.

Felisoni, D. D., & Godoi, A. S. (2018). Cell phone usage and academic performance: An experiment. *Computers & Education*, 117, 175–187.

Fernández-Alonso, R., Suárez-Álvarez, J., & Muñiz, J. (2015). Adolescents' homework performance in mathematics and science: Personal factors and teaching practices. *Journal of Educational Psychology*, 107(4), 1075–1085.

Ferraria, J. R., & Díaz-Moralesb, J. F. (2007). Procrastination: Different time orientations reflect different motives. *Journal of Research in Personality*, 41(3), 707–714.

Fisher, A. V., Godwin, K. E., & Seltman, H. (2014). Visual environment, attention allocation, and learning in young children: When too much of a good thing may be bad. *Psychological Science*, 25(7), 1362–1370.

Fletcher, D., & Sarkar, M. (2016). Mental fortitude training: An evidence-based approach to developing psychological resilience for sustained success. *Journal of Sport Psychology in Action*, 7(3), 135–157.

Foerde, K., & Shohamy, D. (2011). The role of the basal ganglia in learning and memory: Insight from Parkinson's disease. *Neurobiology of Learning and Memory*, 96(4), 624–636.

Forrin, N., & MacLeod, C. (2018). This time it's personal: The memory benefit of hearing oneself. *Memory*, 26(4), 574–579.

Forrin, N. D., Huynh, A. C., Smith, A. C., Cyr, E. N., McLean, D. B., Siklos-Whillans, J., Smilek, D., & MacLeod, C. M. (2021). Attention spreads between students in a learning environment. *Journal of Experimental Psychology: Applied*, 27(2), 276–291.

Fulker, J., Story, M., Mellin, A., Leffert, N., Neumark-Sztainer, D., & French, S. (2006). Family dinner meal frequency and adolescent development: Relationship with developmental assets and high-risk behaviours. *Journal of Adolescent Health*, 39(3), 337–345.

Fuson, K. C. (1987). *Children's Counting and Concepts of Number*. New York: Springer-Verlag.

Gabbert, F., Memon, A., & Allan, K. (2003). Memory conformity: Can eyewitnesses influence each other's memories for an event? *Applied Cognitive Psychology: The Official Journal of the Society for Applied Research in Memory and Cognition*, 17(5), 533–543.

Geary, D. C., van Marle, K., Chu, F. W., Hoard, M. K., & Nugent, L. (2019). Predicting age of becoming a cardinal principle knower. *Journal of Educational Psychology*, 111(2), 256–267.

Gelman, R., & Gallistel, C. R. (2009). *The Child's Understanding of Number*. Cambridge, MA: Harvard University Press.

Gilovich, T., & Savitsky, K. (1999). The spotlight effect and the illusion of transparency: Egocentric assessments of how we are seen by others. *Current Directions in Psychological Science*, 8(6), 165–168.

Gilovich, T., Medvec, V. H., & Savitsky, K. (2000). The spotlight effect in social judgment: An egocentric bias in estimates of the salience of one's own actions and appearance. *Journal of Personality and Social Psychology*, 78(2), 211.

Goldstein, N. J., Cialdini, R. B., & Griskevicius, V. (2008). A room with a viewpoint: Using social norms to motivate environmental conservation in hotels. *Journal of Consumer Research*, 35(3), 472–482.

Green, C. D. (2016). A digital future for the history of psychology? *History of Psychology*, 19(3), 209.

Guilford, J. P. (1967). *The Nature of Human Intelligence*. New York: McGraw-Hill.

Guldvik, M. K., & Kvinnsland, I. (2018). Smarter without smartphones? Effects of mobile phone bans in schools on academic performance, well-being, and bullying. Master's thesis, Norwegian School of Economics.

Gunderson, E., Gripshover, S., Romero, C., Dweck, C., Goldin-Meadow, S., & Levine, S. (2013). Parental praise to 1–3 year olds predicts children's motivation framework 5 years later on. *Child Development*, 84(5), 1526–1541.

Haghbin, M., McCaffrey, A., & Pychyl, T. A. (2012). The complexity of the relation between fear of failure and procrastination. *Journal of Rational-Emotive & Cognitive-Behavior Therapy*, 30(4), 249–263.

Haimovitz, K., & Dweck, C. (2016). What predicts children's fixed and growth mind-sets? Not their parents' view of intelligence but their parents' views of failure. *Psychological Science*, 27(6), 859–869.

Hattie, J., & Timperley, H. (2007). The power of feedback. *Review of Educational Research*, 77(1), 81–112.

Hinze, S. R., & Rapp, D. N. (2014). Retrieval (sometimes) enhances learning: Performance pressure reduces the benefits of retrieval practice. *Applied Cognitive Psychology*, 28(4), 597–606.

Holdsworth, S., Turner, M., & Scott-Young, C. M. (2017). … Not drowning, waving. Resilience and university: A student perspective. *Studies in Higher Education*, 43(11), 1837–1853.

Hsee, C. K., & Hastie, R. (2006). Decision and experience: Why don't we choose what makes us happy? *Trends in Cognitive Sciences*, 10(1), 31–37.

Hui, L., de Bruin, A. B., Donkers, J., & van Merriënboer, J. J. (2021). Does individual performance feedback increase the use of retrieval practice? *Educational Psychology Review*, 33(4), 1835–1857.

Ingram, J., & Elliott, V. (2015). A critical analysis of the role of wait time in classroom interactions and the effects on student and teacher interactional behaviours. *Cambridge Journal of Education*, 46(1), 37–53.

Jang, H. (2008). Supporting students' motivation, engagement, and learning during an uninteresting activity. *Journal of Educational Psychology*, 100(4), 798.

Janssen, C. P., Gould, S. J., Li, S. Y., Brumby, D. P., & Cox, A. L. (2015). Integrating knowledge of multitasking and interruptions across different perspectives and research methods. *International Journal of Human-Computer Studies*, 79, 1–5.

Jefferson, G. (1989). Preliminary notes on a possible metric which provides for a 'standard maximum' silence of approximately one second in conversation. In D. Roger & P. Bull (Eds.), *Conversation: An interdisciplinary perspective* (pp. 166–196). Multilingual Matters.

Jenkins, R. (2017). Using educational neuroscience and psychology to teach science. Part 1. A case study review of cognitive load theory. *School Science Review*, 99, 93–103.

Kahneman, D., Fredrickson, B. L., Schreiber, C. A., & Redelmeier, D. A. (1993). When more pain is preferred to less: Adding a better end. *Psychological Science*, 4(6), 401–405.

Kardas, M., & O'Brien, E. (2018). Easier seen than done: Merely watching others perform can foster an illusion of skill acquisition. *Psychological Science*, 29(4), 521-536.

Karpicke, J. D., Butler, A. C., & Roediger III, H. L. (2009). Metacognitive strategies in student learning: Do students practise retrieval when they study on their own? *Memory*, 17(4), 471-479.

Katzir, M., Emanuel, A., & Liberman, N. (2020). Cognitive performance is enhanced if one knows when the task will end. *Cognition*, 197, 104189.

Kerr, N., & Hertel, G. (2011) The Kohler group motivation gain: How to motivate the 'weak links' in a group. *Social and Personality Psychology Compass*, 5(1), 43-55.

Khattab, N. (2015). Students' aspirations, expectations and school achievement: What really matters? *British Educational Research Journal*, 41(5), 731-748.

Kidd, C., Palmeri, H., & Aslin, R. N. (2013). Rational snacking: Young children's decision-making on the marshmallow task is moderated by beliefs about environmental reliability. *Cognition*, 126(1), 109-114.

King, P. E., Young, M. J., & Behnke, R. R. (1999). Public speaking performance improvement as a function of information processing in immediate and delayed feedback interventions. *Communication Education*, 49(4), 365-374.

Klassen, R. M., Krawchuk, L. L., & Rajani, S. (2008). Academic procrastination of undergraduates: Low self-efficacy to self-regulate predicts higher levels of procrastination. *Contemporary Educational Psychology*, 33(4), 915-931.

Kluger, A. N., & DeNisi, A. (1996). The effects of feedback interventions on performance: A historical review, a meta-analysis, and a preliminary feedback intervention theory. *Psychological Bulletin*, 119(2), 254-284.

Kross, E., Bruehlman-Senecal, E., Park, J., Burson, A., Dougherty, A., Shablack, H., Bremner, R., Moser, J., & Ayduk, O. (2014). Self-talk as a regulatory mechanism: How you do it matters. *Journal of Personality and Social Psychology*, 106(2), 304.

Kruger, J., & Dunning, D. (1999). Unskilled and unaware of it: How difficulties in recognizing one's own incompetence lead to inflated self-assessments. *Journal of Personality and Social Psychology*, 77(6), 1121-1134.

Leahy, W., & Sweller, J. (2004). Cognitive load and the imagination effect. *Applied Cognitive Psychology: The Official Journal of the Society for Applied Research in Memory and Cognition*, 18(7), 857-875.

Le Corre, M. (2013). Children acquire the later-greater principle after the Cardinal Principle. *British Journal of Developmental Psychology*, 32(2), 163-177.

Lee, J., O'Shea, L. J., & Dykes, M. K. (1987). Teacher wait-time: Performance of developmentally delayed and non-delayed young children. *Education and Training in Mental Retardation*, 22(3), 176-184.

LeFevre, J. A., Kamawar, D., Bisanz, J., Skwarchuk, S., Smith-Chant, B., Fast, L., & Watchorn, R. (2008). *Conceptual Knowledge of Counting: How Relevant Is Order Irrelevance?* Austin, TX: Cognitive Science Society ed., 1356-1364.

Lemov, D. (2021). *Teach Like a Champion 3.0: 63 Techniques That Put Students on the Path to College*. John Wiley & Sons.

Lieban, D. (2019). Exploring opportunities for connecting physical and digital resources for mathematics teaching and learning. Doctoral dissertation, Johannes Kepler University.

Lin, P.-H., & Luck, S. J. (2009). The influence of similarity on visual working memory representations. *Visual Cognition*, 17(3), 356-372.

Lin-Siegler, X., Ahn, J. N., Chen, J., Fang, F.-F. A., & Luna-Lucero, M. (2016). Even Einstein struggled: Effects of learning about great scientists' struggles on high school students' motivation to learn science. *Journal of Educational Psychology*, 108(3), 314-328.

Liu, X., Luo, Y., Liu, Z. Z., Yang, Y., Liu, J., & Jia, C. X. (2020). Prolonged mobile phone use is associated with poor academic performance in adolescents. *Cyberpsychology, Behavior, and Social Networking*, 23(5), 303-311.

Mark, G., Gudith, D., & Klocke, U. (2008, April). The cost of interrupted work: more speed and stress. In *Proceedings of the SIGCHI Conference on Human Factors in Computing Systems* (pp. 107-110).

Martin, A. J., Colmar, S. H., Davey, L. A., & Marsh, H. W. (2010). Longitudinal modelling of academic buoyancy and motivation: Do the 5Cs hold up over time? *British Journal of Educational Psychology*, 80(3), 473-496.

Maslow, A. H. (1943). A theory of human motivation. *Psychological Review*, 50(4), 370-396.

Mayer, R. E., & Anderson, R. B. (1991). Animations need narrations: An experimental test of a dual-coding hypothesis. *Journal of Educational Psychology*, 83(4), 484-490.

McCrea, P. (2019). *Learning: What Is It, and How Might We Catalyse It?* Ambition Institute.

Metcalfe, J., & Mieleb, D. B. (2014). Hypercorrection of high confidence errors: Prior testing both enhances delayed performance and blocks the return of the errors. *Journal of Applied Research in Memory and Cognition*, 3(3), 189-197.

Miller, C., & Krizan, Z. (2016) Walking facilitates positive affect (even when expecting the opposite). *Emotion*, 16(5), 775-785.

Moreno, R., & Mayer, R. E. (2000). A coherence effect in multimedia learning: The case for minimizing irrelevant sounds in the design of multimedia instructional messages. *Journal of Educational Psychology*, 92(1), 117.

Mueller, C. M., & Dweck, C. S. (1998). Praise for intelligence can undermine children's motivation and performance. *Journal of Personality and Social Psychology*, 75(1), 33.

Mueller, P., & Oppenheimer, D. (2014). The pen is mightier than the keyboard: Advantages of longhand over laptop note taking. *Psychological Science*, 25(6), 1159-1168.

Murre, J. M., & Dros, J. (2015). Replication and analysis of Ebbinghaus' forgetting curve. *PLoS ONE*, 10(7), e0120644.

Naujoks, N., Harder, B., & Händel, M. (2022). Testing pays off twice: Potentials of practice tests and feedback regarding exam performance and judgment accuracy. *Metacognition and Learning*, 17(2), 1-20.

Nestojko, J., Bui, D., Kornell, N., & Bjork, E. (2014). Expecting to teach enhances learning and organization of knowledge in free recall of text passages. *Memory & Cognition*, 42(7), 1038-1048.

Ng, S. F., Hassan, N. S. I. C., Nor, N. H. M., & Malek, N. A. A. (2017). The relationship between smartphone use and academic performance: A case of students in a Malaysian tertiary institution. *Malaysian Online Journal of Educational Technology*, 5(4), 58-70.

Nie, P., Ma, W., & Sousa-Poza, A. (2021). The relationship between smartphone use and subjective well-being in rural China. *Electronic Commerce Journal*, 21(4), 983-1009.

Norton, M., Mochon, D., & Ariely, D. (2011). The 'IKEA effect': When labor leads to love. Harvard Business School, 1-33.

Ostrow, K., Heffernan, N., Heffernan, C., & Peterson, Z. (2015, June). Blocking vs. interleaving: Examining single-session effects within middle school math homework. In *International Conference on Artificial Intelligence in Education* (pp. 338-347). Cham: Springer.

Parker, P. D., Marsh, H. W., Thoemmes, F., & Biddle, N. (2019). The negative year in school effect: Extending scope and strengthening causal claims. *Journal of Educational Psychology*, 111(1), 118-130.

Parson, J., Adler, T., & Kaczala, C. (1982). Socialization of achievement attitudes and beliefs: Parental influences. *Child Development*, 53(2), 310-321.

Parsons, S., & Hallam, S. (2014). The impact of streaming on attainment at age seven: Evidence from the Millennium Cohort Study. *Oxford Review of Education*, 40(5), 567-589.

Pashler, H., Bain, P., Bottge, B., Graesser, A., Koedinger, K., McDaniel, M., & Metcalfe, J. (2007). *Organizing Instruction and Study to Improve Student Learning*. National Center for Education Research.

Pashler, H., McDaniel, M., Rohrer, D., & Bjork, R. (2008). Learning styles concepts and evidence. *Psychological Science in the Public Interest*, 9(3), 105-119.

Patel, R., Liu, R., & Koedinger, K. (2016). When to block versus interleave practice? Evidence against teaching fraction addition before fraction multiplication. Proceedings of the 38th Annual Meeting of the Cognitive Science Society.

Pauk, W. (1962). *How to Study in College*. Boston: Houghton Mifflin.

Paunesku, D., Walton, G. M., Romero, C., Smith, E. N., Yeager, D. S., & Dweck, C. S. (2015). Mind-set interventions are a scalable treatment for academic underachievement. *Psychological Science*, 26(6), 784-793.

Pekrun, R. (2017). Emotion and achievement during adolescence. *Child Development Perspectives*, 11(3), 215-221.

Pekrun, R., Lichtenfeld, S., Marsh, H., Murayama, K., & Goetz, T. (2017). Achievement emotions and academic performance: Longitudinal models of reciprocal effects. *Child Development*, 88(5), 1653-1670.

Peper, R. J., & Mayer, R. E. (1986). Generative effects of note-taking during science lectures. *Journal of Educational Psychology*, 78(1), 34-38.

Perham, N., & Currie, H. (2014). Does listening to preferred music improve reading comprehension performance? *Applied Cognitive Psychology*, 28(2), 279-284.

Perry, J., Lundie, D., & Golder, G. (2019). Metacognition in schools: What does the literature suggest about the effectiveness of teaching metacognition in schools? *Educational Review*, 71(4), 483-500.

Perry, T., Lea, R., Jørgensen, C. R., Cordingley, P., Shapiro, K., & Youdell, D. (2021). *Cognitive Science in the Classroom*. Education Endowment Foundation (EEF).

Peterson, L., & Peterson, M. J. (1959). Short-term retention of individual verbal items. *Journal of Experimental Psychology*, 58(3), 193-198.

Pham, L.. & Taylor, S. (1999). From thought to action: Effects of process- versus outcome-based mental simulations on performance. *Personality and Social Psychology Bulletin*, 25(2), 250-260.

Pires, A. C., González Perilli, F., Bakała, E., Fleisher, B., Sansone, G., & Marichal, S. (2019, September). Building blocks of mathematical learning: Virtual and tangible manipulatives lead to different strategies in number composition. *Frontiers in Education*, 4, 81. Frontiers Media SA.

Pomerance, L., Greenberg, J., & Walsh, K. (2016). *Learning about Learning: What Every New Teacher Needs to Know*. National Council on Teacher Quality.

Porter, G., Hampshire, K., Milner, J., Munthali, A., Robson, E., De Lannoy, A., ... & Abane, A. (2015). Mobile phones and education in Sub-Saharan Africa: From youth practice to public policy. *Journal of International Development*, 28(1), 22-39.

Pressley, M., McDaniel, M. A., Turnure, J. E., Wood, E., & Ahmad, M. (1987). Generation and precision of elaboration: Effects on intentional and incidental learning. *Journal of Experimental Psychology: Learning, Memory, and Cognition*, 13(2), 291.

Quent, J. A., Henson, R. N., & Greve, A. (2021). A predictive account of how novelty influences declarative memory. *Neurobiology of Learning and Memory*, 179, 107382.

Quigley, A., Muijs, D., & Stringer, E. (2018). Metacognition and self-regulated learning: Guidance report. Education Endowment Foundation (EEF).

Rattan, A., Good, C., & Dweck, C. S. (2012). "It's ok – Not everyone can be good at math": Instructors with an entity theory comfort (and demotivate) students. *Journal of Experimental Social Psychology*, 48(3), 731-737.

Rebetez, M. M. L., Rochat, L., Barsics, C., & Van der Linden, M. (2016). Procrastination as a self-regulation failure: The role of inhibition, negative affect, and gender. *Personality and Individual Differences*, 101, 435-439.

Rebetez, M., Rochat, L., Barsics, C., & Van der Linden, M. (2018). Procrastination as a self-regulation failure: The role of impulsivity and intrusive thoughts. *Psychological Reports*, 121(1), 26-41.

Reeve, J., Jang, H., Carrell, D., Jeon, S., & Barch, J. (2004). Enhancing students' engagement by increasing teachers' autonomy support. *Motivation and Emotion*, 28(2), 147-169.

Richland, L. E., Kornell, N., & Kao, L. S. (2009). The pretesting effect: Do unsuccessful retrieval attempts enhance learning? *Journal of Experimental Psychology: Applied*, 15(3), 243-257.

Rittle-Johnson, B., Star, J. R., & Durkin, K. (2009). The importance of prior knowledge when comparing examples: Influences on conceptual and procedural knowledge of equation solving. *Journal of Educational Psychology*, 101(4), 836.

Robins, R., & Pals, J. (2002). Implicit self-theories in the academic domain: Implications for goal orientation, attributions, affect, and self-esteem change. *Self and Identity*, 1(4), 313-336.

Rock, D. (2009). *Your Brain at Work: Strategies for Overcoming Distraction, Regaining Focus, and Working Smarter All Day Long*. Harper Business.

Roediger III, H. L., & Karpicke, J. D. (2006). Test-enhanced learning: Taking memory tests improves long-term retention. *Psychological Science*, 17(3), 249-255.

Roediger III, H. L., Putnam, A. L., & Smith, M. A. (2011). Ten benefits of testing and their applications to educational practice. *Psychology of Learning and Motivation*, 55, 1-36.

Rohrer, D. (2012). Interleaving helps students distinguish among similar concepts. *Educational Psychology Review*, 24(3), 355-367.

Rohrer, D., & Taylor, K. (2007). The shuffling of mathematics problems improves learning. *Instructional Science*, 35, 481-498.

Rohrer, D., Dedrick, R. F., Hartwig, M. K., & Cheung, C.-N. (2020). A randomized controlled trial of interleaved mathematics practice. *Journal of Educational Psychology*, 112(1), 40-52.

Rosenshine, B. (2012). Principles of instruction: Research-based strategies that all teachers should know. *American Educator*, 36(1), 12-39.

Rosenthal, R., & Jacobson, L. (1968). Pygmalion in the classroom. *The Urban Review*, 3(1), 16-20.

Rowe, M. B. (1986). Wait time: Slowing down may be a way of speeding up! *Journal of Teacher Education*, 37(1), 43-50.

Rubinstein, J. S., Meyer, D. E., & Evans, J. E. (2001). Executive control of cognitive processes in task switching. *Journal of Experimental Psychology: Human Perception and Performance*, 27(4), 763-797.

San Cristóbal, J. R., Carral, L., Diaz, E., Fraguela, J. A., & Iglesias, G. (2018). Complexity and project management: A general overview. *Complexity*, 2018, 1-10.

Sarnecka, B. W., & Carey, S. (2008). How counting represents number: What children must learn and when they learn it. *Cognition*, 108(3), 662-674.

Schmeck, A., Mayer, R. E., Opfermann, M., Pfeiffer, V., & Leutner, D. (2014). Drawing pictures during learning from scientific text: Testing the generative drawing effect and the prognostic drawing effect. *Contemporary Educational Psychology*, 39(4), 275-286.

Sebastian, C., Viding, E., Williams, K. D., & Blakemore, S. J. (2010). Social brain development and the affective consequences of ostracism in adolescence. *Brain and Cognition*, 72(1), 134-145.

Senechal, M., & LeFevre, J. (2002). Parental involvement in the development of children's reading skill: A five-year longitudinal study. *Child Development*, 73(2), 445-460.

Shoda, Y., Mischel, W., & Peake, P. K. (1990). Predicting adolescent cognitive and self-regulatory competencies from preschool delay of gratification: Identifying diagnostic conditions. *Developmental Psychology*, 26(6), 978.

Short, M. A., Gradisar, M., Lack, L. C., Wright, H. R., & Chatburn, A. (2013). Estimating adolescent sleep patterns: Parent reports versus adolescent self-report surveys, sleep diaries, and actigraphy. *Nature and Science of Sleep*, 5, 23-26.

Sirois, F. M. (2007). "I'll look after my health, later": A replication and extension of the procrastination-health model with community-dwelling adults. *Personality and Individual Differences*, 43(1), 15-26.

Skipper, Y., & Douglas, K. (2015). The influence of teacher feedback on children's perceptions of student–teacher relationships. *British Journal of Educational Psychology*, 85(3), 276-288.

Smith, A. M., Floerke, V. A., & Thomas, A. K. (2016). Retrieval practice protects memory against acute stress. *Science*, 354(6315), 1046-1048.

Sparrow, B., Liu, J., & Wegner, D. M. (2011). Google effects on memory: Cognitive consequences of having information at our fingertips. *Science*, 333(6043), 776-778.

Spillane, J. P., Shirrell, M., & Adhikari, S. (2018). Constructing "Experts" among peers: Educational infrastructure, test data, and teachers' interactions about teaching. *Educational Evaluation and Policy Analysis*, 40(4), 586-612.

Stahl, R. J. (1994). Using "think-time" and "wait-time" skillfully in the classroom. *ERIC Digest*.

Stiglic, N., & Viner, R. M. (2019). Effects of screentime on the health and well-being of children and adolescents: A systematic review of reviews. *BMJ open*, 9(1), 1-15.

Sweller, J., Ayres, P., & Kalyuga, S. (2011). The Goal-Free Effect. *Cognitive Load Theory*, 89, 98.

Sweller, J., van Merriënboer, J. J. G., & Paas, F. (2019). Cognitive architecture and instructional design: 20 years later. *Educational Psychology Review*, 31(2), 261-292.

Terman, L. M. (1959). The gifted group at mid-life; Thirty-five years' follow-up of the superior child. *Genetic Studies of Genius*, vol. V.

Thomson, D. (2017, March 3). Getting older quicker. FFT Education Datalab. https://ffteducationdatalab.org.uk/2017/03/getting-older-quicker/.

Thornton, B., Faires, A., Robbins, M., & Rollins, E. (2014). The mere presence of a cell phone may be distracting: Implications for attention and task performance. *Social Psychology*, 45(6), 479-488.

Tobin, K. (1987). The role of wait time in higher cognitive level learning. *Review of Educational Research*, 57(1), 69-95.

Topor, D. R., Keane, S. P., Shelton, T. L., & Calkins, S. D. (2010). Parent involvement and student academic performance: A multiple mediational analysis. *Journal of Prevention & Intervention in the Community*, 38(3), 183-197.

Toste, J. R., Didion, L., Peng, P., Filderman, M. J., & McClelland, A. M. (2020). A meta-analytic review of the relations between motivation and reading achievement for K-12 students. *Review of Educational Research*, 90(3), 420-456.

Tsay, C. J., & Banaji, M. R. (2011). Naturals and strivers: Preferences and beliefs about sources of achievement. *Journal of Experimental Social Psychology*, 47(2), 460-465.

Twenge, J. M., & Campbell, W. K. (2018). Associations between screen time and lower psychological well-being among children and adolescents: Evidence from a population-based study. *Preventive Medicine Reports*, 12, 271-283.

Uttl, B., White, C. A., & Gonzalez, D. W. (2017). Meta-analysis of faculty's teaching effectiveness: Student evaluation of teaching ratings and student learning are not related. *Studies in Educational Evaluation*, 54, 22-42.

Vasilev, M. R., Kirkby, J. A., & Angele, B. (2018). Auditory distraction during reading: A Bayesian meta-analysis of a continuing controversy. *Perspectives on Psychological Science*, 13(5), 567-597.

Vaughn, K. E., Fitzgerald, G., Hood, D., Migneault, K., & Krummen, K. (2022). The effect of hint strength on the benefits of retrieval practice. *Applied Cognitive Psychology*, 36(2), 468-476.

Vergauwe, J., Wille, B., Feys, M., De Fruyt, F., & Anseel, F. (2015). Fear of being exposed: The trait-relatedness of the impostor phenomenon and its relevance in the work context. *Journal of Business and Psychology*, 30(3), 565-581.

Walker, M. P., & Van der Helm, E. (2009). Overnight therapy? The role of sleep in emotional brain processing. *Psychological Bulletin*, 135(5), 731.

Wammes, J., Boucher, P., Seli, P., Cheyne, J., & Smilek, D. (2016). Mind wandering during lectures I: Changes in rates across an entire semester. *Scholarship of Teaching and Learning in Psychology*, 2(1), 13-32.

Wang, Y., Jones, B. F., & Wang, D. (2019). Early-career setback and future career impact. *Nature Communications*, 10(1), 1-10.

Wannarka, R., & Ruhl, K. (2008). Seating arrangements that promote positive academic and behavioural outcomes: A review of empirical research. *Support for Learning*, 23(2), 89-83.

Wegner, D., Schneider, D., Carter, S., & White, T. (1987). Paradoxical effects of thought suppression. *Journal of Personality and Social Psychology*, 53(1), 5-13.

Weinstein, Y., Madan, C. R., & Sumeracki, M. A. (2018). Teaching the science of learning. *Cognitive Research: Principles and Implications*, 3(1).

Weisberg, D. S., Keil, F. C., Goodstein, J., Rawson, E., & Gray, J. R. (2008). The seductive allure of neuroscience explanations. *Journal of Cognitive Neuroscience*, 20(3), 470-477.

Wesnes, K. A., Pincock, C., Richardson, D., Helm, G., & Hails, S. (2003). Breakfast reduces declines in attention and memory over the morning in schoolchildren. *Appetite*, 41(3), 329-331.

Wheldall, K., & Lam, Y. Y. (1987). Rows versus tables. II. The effects of two classroom seating arrangements on classroom disruption rate, on-task behaviour and teacher behaviour in three special school classes. *Educational Psychology*, 7(4), 303-312.

Wilson, A., & Ross, M. (2001). From chump to champ: People's appraisals of their earlier and present selves. *Journal of Personality and Social Psychology*, 80(4), 572-584.

Winskel, H., Kim, T. H., Kardash, L., & Belic, I. (2019). Smartphone use and study behavior: A Korean and Australian comparison. *Heliyon*, 5(7).

Wood, B., Rea, M. S., Plitnick, B., & Figueiro, M. G. (2013). Light level and duration of exposure determine the impact of self-luminous tablets on melatonin suppression. *Applied Ergonomics*, 44(2), 237-240.

Wypych, M., Matuszewski, J., & Dragan, W. Ł. (2018). Roles of impulsivity, motivation, and emotion regulation in procrastination – path analysis and comparison between students and non-students. *Frontiers in Psychology*, 9, 891.

Xu, K. M., Koorn, P., De Koning, B., Skuballa, I. T., Lin, L., Henderikx, M., ... & Paas, F. (2021). A growth mindset lowers perceived cognitive load and improves learning: Integrating motivation to cognitive load. *Journal of Educational Psychology*, 113(6), 1177.

Yan, V. X., Thai, K. P., & Bjork, R. A. (2014). Habits and beliefs that guide self-regulated learning: Do they vary with mindset? *Journal of Applied Research in Memory and Cognition*, 3(3), 140-152.

Zhao, L., Heyman, G., Chen, L., & Lee, K. (2017). Telling young children they have a reputation for being smart promotes cheating. *Developmental Science*, 21(3), e12585.